July 5, 2021

To Brian and Sherry, a
very civil couple,

Civility rules!

Civility
GEORGE WASHINGTON'S
110 RULES FOR TODAY

STEVEN MICHAEL SELZER

Andrews McMeel
PUBLISHING®

In memory of Nathan Selzer, my father, and Walter and Betty Heafitz, parents of my very civil wife, Adrianne. All of them treated everyone with respect.

CONTENTS

INTRODUCTION

Rudeness. Crudeness. Thoughtlessness. Today, uncivil behavior is everywhere. From the boss who publicly chews out her assistant, to the driver who barrels dangerously down the highway, to the sports fan who yells obscenities at the ball game, there is little doubt that we live in an increasingly barbaric world. But this need not be the case.

Civility, of course, goes beyond good manners. It is about conduct where people treat each other with respect, courtesy, empathy, and consideration in all aspects of their lives. The concept that underlies civility is an awareness of how an action or inaction has an effect on other individuals and the larger society, with a view toward maximizing well-being and minimizing harm. And that also includes our treatment of the natural world. Helen Keller summed it up well when she said, "Life is an exciting business, and most exciting when it is lived for others."

The desire for a more civil world seems to be on the minds of almost everyone these days. We all recognize that it would be much more pleasant if the prevailing culture was a civil one.

I have a theory that civility is like a pendulum: societies seem to swing back and forth between extremes. Hopefully, the pendulum can swing back, toward better treatment of one another. Certainly the vast majority of Americans want to see it happen. Civil behavior is contagious. It can spread like a movement.

But doing the civil thing in every situation can be confusing in these modern times of great change. We ought to consider our need for some guidance. Sometimes, in order to move forward, we need to take a long look back.

Enter George Washington. Among his many fine qualities, he was a person of great integrity, courage, and judgment who remains one of the most revered figures in the history of our country. Washington was a person of strong character, which is closely linked to civility. General Washington was a great leader, known for his fair and inspiring treatment of his soldiers. And President Washington set the tone for our democracy, serving the country as our first president after being unanimously chosen.

At the end of Washington's two terms, many people wanted to anoint him king—as was common in many countries in those days. Instead, he gave the power back to the people. For good reason, some historians have dubbed him "the indispensable man." It is probable that without him we would not have a democratic country.

What is less commonly known about George Washington is that, at the age of fourteen, the father of our country wrote down 110 principles for personal conduct initially titled *Rules of Civility and Decent Behaviour in Company and Conversation*. Washington copied the rules from a manual composed by French Jesuits in 1595, apparently as a school handwriting exercise. Maybe he did this in part to emulate the civil person he most respected, his father Augustine, who died when Washington was eleven years old. Whether he originated or adapted the rules is not important; the exercise of writing them down and learning them is now regarded as a formative influence in the development of his character. Washington valued the rules so much that he carried the list of guidelines with him throughout his life.

Although the rules were written more than 250 years ago, they remain fundamentally pertinent and valuable. In this book, as Washington's old rules are brought to bear on modern problems, sticky social situations, and twenty-first-century media, it becomes clear just how deeply the way we treat each other affects us all.

A quick note on these rules: I've tried to preserve their original language to the fullest extent possible. It is important to mention that in Washington's time, all generic pronouns and nouns were in the masculine. This language is retained because a change to modern practice would have altered the text's authenticity and character. Of course, the rules and the comments following them apply to both men and women alike. In some instances, however, the more archaic words of Washington's rules have been "translated" to their modern equivalents to aid understanding. These changes are shown in brackets.

I must stress that this book is not political. The original rules don't have a partisan slant, and that's because civility applies to people of all viewpoints. It does not matter what a person's political bent is; there is something in Washington's rules for everyone. But their broader application does, importantly, apply to politicians. Civility is a universal concept.

The cultural ramifications of the way we treat one another in private and in public have never been more significant than they are today. In a world where everything is increasingly fast, our impatience fuels our entitlement and need for immediate gratification. It's easier than ever to withhold from others the time they deserve. It has now been made very clear, however, that more and more people crave the return of, or movement in the direction toward, greater civility in modern times. We can make it happen.

I hope I am not taking extraordinary license in stating what I believe George Washington would say today. I do so modestly. With every entry in the book, I endeavor to stay true to his rules while keeping in mind their modern relevance. This great man's guidance, contemporized, can hopefully help us get a better grip on our current situation so we can move forward in a positive direction.

THE **RULES**

Rule 1

EVERY ACTION DONE IN COMPANY OUGHT TO

BE DONE WITH SOME SIGN OF RESPECT TO

THOSE THAT ARE PRESENT.

Everybody wants and deserves respect, which is the cornerstone of civility. In addition to self-respect, there is respect for others. Being considerate uplifts us all. Appreciating pride and human dignity is essential.

The problem is that respect seems to be in short supply these days. The late Aretha Franklin's well-known song emphatically spells out what we need: R-E-S-P-E-C-T. It applies to all human endeavors.

It's up to all of us to increase the world's supply of respect. As you go through your day, consider all the people you come in contact with, from the trash collector to your coworkers to the pierced and tattooed teenager down the street. Honor their individuality, abilities, and humanity, and let them know in some way that you appreciate them. A wave and a smile will do. In looking at someone, remember the adage, "You can't judge a book by its cover." Some clichés are cliché for a reason.

Consider the job of the person who cleans the public bathrooms you use or returns the shopping carts you push. If you see them working, pause to briefly tell them that they do a good job or at least give them a nod. That recognition will be appreciated. They are not invisible.

Your mail carrier and newspaper delivery person, if you have one, work in all weather conditions. They should be treated with a nice note of thanks or even a gift during the holidays. Hopefully, you are grateful for their services. These days you may not know your mail carrier's or newspaper delivery person's name, but you can learn it by simply calling your local post or newspaper office—and then leave your envelope with a note to him or her in the mailbox, or simply wait until they swing by. These hardworking people deserve recognition. And you will feel good about it. Putting yourself in their shoes for a bit will allow you to be a more sensitive person.

Our need for respect does not only apply to people; it is a positive regard for the worth of something as well. It applies to nature and the environment. Respect applies to country and to responsible civic, social, educational, religious, and government institutions. Respect should be accorded to dutiful authorities, which include parents, grandparents, other family members, teachers, judges, babysitters, au pairs, caretakers, firefighters, and well-trained police officers, which are the overwhelming majority.

As a matter of sportsmanship, there should be respect for the rules of the game, teammates and opposition players, referees, and coaches. The fans need to show respect by rooting with appropriate conduct that is not out of control. They should praise not only their own team but the players on the other team as well.

There must importantly be respect for the rule of law, which codifies ethical standards. "Let reverence for the laws," Abraham Lincoln said, "be breathed by every American mother to the lisping babe that prattles on her lap; let it be taught in the schools, seminaries, and in colleges; let it be written in primers, spelling books, and in almanacs; let it be preached from the pulpit, proclaimed in legislative halls, and enforced in courts of justice. And, in short, let it become the political religion of the nation."

Communicating Respect

Frank was leaving the supermarket with his shopping cart of groceries. It was a cold night. He came upon an employee who was hauling a long line of carts back to the store. Frank paused and told the man that he respected the hard work that he was doing. The employee lit up and said, "Thank you, sir."

This man was not invisible to Frank. He was simply showing thanks to a man who had an all-too-often thankless job.

Civility comes in small but thoughtful acts, with people treating each other with respect, empathy, courtesy, and consideration. It is being polite to everyone, even those who are rude to you.

Why? Because you take the high road. Civility is humility in all you say and do.

Address to the Continental Congress, June 16, 1775 (when informed he had been chosen to be general and commander in chief of the American forces):

"THO' I AM TRULY SENSIBLE OF

THE HIGH HONOR DONE ME

IN THE APPOINTMENT, YET I

FEEL GREAT DISTRESS, FROM A

CONSCIOUSNESS THAT MY ABILITIES

AND MILITARY EXPERIENCE MAY

NOT BE EQUAL TO THE EXTENSIVE

AND IMPORTANT TRUST."

G Washington

Rule 2

WHEN IN COMPANY, PUT NOT YOUR HANDS

TO ANY PART OF THE BODY NOT USUALLY

DISCOVERED.

For shame! If we go back 250 years, the word "discovered" in this context meant "displayed." No one wants to see this, and it should not be talked about either. The rule applies to rock stars as well.

And even when you are not in company, do not send images or videos of parts of your body "not usually discovered." Remember, once an image or video is on the internet, it is there for all time. Even seemingly private messages are often stored in perpetuity by tech companies. Best to avoid altogether.

And perhaps most importantly, this rule applies to putting your unwelcome hands on others.

Rule 3

SHEW [SHOW] NOTHING TO YOUR FRIEND THAT

MAY AFFRIGHT HIM.

This rule is suspended during Halloween.

Just as friends don't let friends engage in dangerous activities, a friend doesn't make another friend's skin crawl, hair stand on end, or heart beat rapidly. Frightening someone can be an inconsiderate exercise of power. A thoughtful, civilized person thinks twice before bringing together the unsuspecting with, for example, large spiders and reptiles. For those who want to indulge in frightening stuff, there are plenty of options, like horror films and roller coasters.

Carefully consider who might see the gross jokes, pictures, images, and videos you send or post on social media. And only send or post these to personal accounts, not business accounts, of your family and friends.

Many businesses frown on their employees using work e-mail for personal communications. This applies especially to jokes or comments that have the potential to violate the company's rules against the many forms of harassment.

Rule 4

IN THE PRESENCE OF OTHERS, SING NOT TO

YOURSELF WITH A HUMMING NOISE, NOR DRUM

WITH YOUR FINGERS OR FEET.

It is pleasing to know that this isn't a new problem. Do not annoy or distract. Letting loud music blare from your open apartment window, phone, or car radio, for example, is inconsiderate. The same can be said for talking and fidgeting during movies or speaking loudly at a library, meeting, yoga class, art gallery, or place of worship.

There are modern exceptions to this rule. Stomping, clapping, applauding, and cheering while rooting for your favorite team is acceptable in our sports-oriented culture, as long as the words do not turn profane. The same goes for your conduct at a concert or show, if suitable, depending on the type of performance.

Rule 5

IF YOU COUGH, SNEEZE, SIGH, OR YAWN, DO IT
NOT LOUD BUT PRIVATELY; AND SPEAK NOT IN
YOUR YAWNING, BUT PUT YOUR HANDKERCHIEF
OR HAND BEFORE YOUR FACE AND TURN ASIDE.

Although sometimes we are taken by surprise and cannot avoid
transgressing, these are practices we should have learned in
preschool. Sharing (another preschool lesson) does not apply
to germs, so use a hanky or a tissue—or even your sleeve if you
must—and turn aside. Good manners and good hygiene go hand
in hand. And if you do erupt in an explosive event, cover your
mouth and excuse yourself. A yawn may be involuntary, but you
can avoid speaking at the same time.

Rule 6

SLEEP NOT WHEN OTHERS SPEAK, SIT NOT

WHEN OTHERS STAND, SPEAK NOT WHEN YOU

SHOULD HOLD YOUR PEACE, WALK NOT ON

WHEN OTHERS STOP.

This rule covers a lot of ground.

Sleeping in the back of class, for example, shows little respect for the one up front and practically guarantees you a poor grade. You will miss the point of the class, which is, of course, to learn. Remember that knowledge is power.

There was a young man who slept through a video at his required alcohol education class. The purpose of attentively completing the course was that he would no longer be ignorant about the dangers and consequences of drinking and driving. He would no longer be a menace on the roads. We are all responsible for our own behavior.

Sitting while others stand is generally okay if not too awkward. Speaking when you should hold your peace may get you a piece of someone's mind. If you sense, after a brief greeting, when not to speak, seatmates on your bus, plane, or train are likely to be appreciative. The last point of the rule is that, if you walk on when others stop, you'll soon be walking alone.

When you are with other people, either socially or at work, unless there is an opportunity to break away from those people, avoid spending time on your cell phone. Put your phone away and give them your full attention. The screen addiction must be overcome.

Rule 7

PUT NOT OFF YOUR CLOTHS IN THE PRESENCE

OF OTHERS, NOR GO OUT OF YOUR CHAMBER

HALF DREST [DRESSED].

Clothes may not make the man (or woman), but taking them off indiscriminately may be your undoing, especially if—again—a photo ends up online. Once an image is out in the world, there is no getting it back.

Even casual Fridays and, for that matter, casual clothes at the office have their limits. Dress codes and uniforms at some jobs, schools, and summer camps may make sense.

The larger point is to be properly dressed depending upon the circumstances or activity. People should not be judged by their appearance but sometimes they are. Be considerate of others and use your discretion when evaluating what clothing is appropriate for a given social or business situation.

Rule 8

AT PLAY AND AT FIRE, IT'S GOOD MANNERS TO
GIVE PLACE TO THE LAST COMER, AND AFFECT
NOT TO SPEAK LOUDER THAN ORDINARY.

Arriving last is always a bit uncomfortable so it's generous to include a latecomer in an activity that has already started, be it around the campfire or in a sports or card game. Welcome others as you would like to be welcomed. Last in a line, however, is always last—especially at the supermarket, bus stop, and movie theater.

Speaking loudly still offends all but the hard of hearing. Turn down the volume and use a moderate tone, except in an emergency.

When writing a text, e-mail, or post on social media, it is preferred that you avoid using all capital letters. It gives the impression that you are shouting at the recipient and could get you eliminated from a forum or unfollowed on social media. It can also be seen as rude. If you want to gain attention, limit your use of ALL CAPS to one or two words. ALL CAPS are okay in an emergency.

At the Supermarket

Pam was shopping for a few items at the supermarket one afternoon. She was in the "fifteen items or less" line behind two young men. Pam was pleased that the express line was open because she was in a hurry and the other lines were very long.

The men in front of her were furiously unloading their cart when the cashier noticed that they had many more than fifteen items. She immediately turned toward the men, pointed up to the large sign, and politely but firmly said, "Oh no, this is the express line."

The cashier then quietly listened to the young men when they claimed that they had missed the sign. Then they pointed out that they'd started unloading their groceries. "I'm afraid the rule is the rule," the cashier then told them in a normal tone of voice. "It wouldn't be fair to the people behind you." She then directed them to the next line over.

Pam complimented the cashier, moved up, and was quickly back at her car with a smile on her face.

What good is a reasonable rule if it is not enforced?

Rule 9

SPIT NOT INTO THE FIRE, NOR STOOP LOW
BEFORE IT. NEITHER PUT YOUR HANDS INTO THE
FLAMES TO WARM THEM, NOR SET YOUR FEET
UPON THE FIRE, ESPECIALLY IF THERE BE MEAT
BEFORE IT.

Spitting into the fire does not seem to be a problem anymore.
Nevertheless, this rule can easily be translated from the
eighteenth century. It instructs us to share the comforts. Don't
block the heat or the view. Be aware of those around you.
Don't sit in front of someone in a near-empty movie theater,
concert hall, classroom, or auditorium. Watch out for the other
celebrants on blankets at a Fourth of July celebration. Consider
those waiting in line to use the restroom and do not circumvent.
Community is created by sharing.

Walking Downtown

Joan and Jason were enjoying shopping downtown on a sunny afternoon. As they were walking, a middle-aged man slightly ahead of them spat a large glob on the sidewalk in front of them. They looked at each other in disgust.

"How lovely," Joan said to Jason.

"And hygienic," Jason agreed.

Then an interesting thing happened. The man spat a second time, but while still in the air, the missile was lifted by a gust of wind. It landed on the face of the spitter with a splat. They agreed that justice had been done.

Rule 10

WHEN YOU SIT DOWN, KEEP YOUR FEET FIRM

AND EVEN, WITHOUT PUTTING ONE ON THE

OTHER OR CROSSING THEM.

The arrangement of your feet is no longer a matter of civility provided they are not placed upon the furniture without permission. Cross your legs if it pleases you.

Rule 11

SHIFT NOT YOURSELF IN THE SIGHT OF OTHERS

NOR GNAW YOUR NAILS.

Shift all you like but back off on your fingernails. The disgusting and unsanitary habit of nail biting, which evidently existed 250 years ago, ought to have ended by now. Nail clippers were clearly invented for this purpose. And do it in private. Let's add cracking knuckles to the endangered-habit list as well. And nose picking. It is so simple to have a tissue handy.

Rule 12

SHAKE NOT THE HEAD, FEET, OR LEGS, ROWL

[ROLL] NOT THE EYS, LIFT NOT ONE EYEBROW

HIGHER THAN THE OTHER, WRY NOT THE

MOUTH, AND BEDEW NO MAN'S FACE WITH

YOUR SPITTLE BY APPROACHING TOO NEAR HIM

WHEN YOU SPEAK.

Physical comments speak as loudly as verbal ones. Make every effort to hide feelings you might be tempted to express with parts of your body.

Don't use your face to register disagreement with someone's legitimate opinion. Do not pretend to tolerate differences of lifestyle while your body shows disapproval. And when you dispute, mind your saliva. Even the most vigorous of discussions should not result in a shower on your opponent's face. Stand back and swallow often.

Believe it or not, our feelings do come through in e-mail, texting, and other types of social media, whether intentional or not. The way in which we word our statements is critical to ensuring our intended message gets across when the receiving person can't see our face, notice our body language, or hear our tone of voice.

Use emojis sparingly, especially in professional contexts. Not everyone understands them the same way and, depending on how you worded your statement, the emoji may change your intended meaning.

Rule 13

KILL NO VERMIN, AS FLEAS, LICE, TICKS, ETC.,

IN THE SIGHT OF OTHERS. IF YOU SEE ANY

FILTH OR THICK SPITTLE, PUT YOUR FOOT

DEXTEROUSLY UPON IT; IF IT BE UPON THE

CLOTHS OF YOUR COMPANIONS, PUT IT OFF

PRIVATELY; AND IF IT BE UPON YOUR OWN

CLOTHS, RETURN THANKS TO HIM WHO PUTS

IT OFF.

We might think that, not being exterminators, we would have little use for this advice. But once we get past the odious vermin, the lesson is clearly valuable. When you help someone, do it quietly, without fanfare and without expecting anything in return.

Do acknowledge those who help you. It's nearly impossible to overuse the words "please," "thank you," "excuse me," and "you're welcome." The tone of your voice enhances your expression of appreciation.

Please heed this simple advice all of the time. Thank you.

The Flight Attendant

We were aloft. The flight attendant, who was beginning to serve beverages, kindly asked the passengers what they would like to drink. When she arrived at our row, the gentleman sitting next to me said, "Ginger ale, please." I asked, "May I have a Coke, please?" She smiled as she handed us our drinks. We each thanked her, and she replied, "You're welcome."

She then turned to the woman on the other side of the aisle, who was reading a newspaper, and asked her what she would like to drink. Without looking up, the passenger brusquely responded, "Apple juice." The flight attendant looked at the woman, then slowly poured the juice into a cup and stood there holding it. After a few moments the woman looked up. Nothing was said but it was obvious the drink was not going to be served. Finally, the woman came to her civil senses. She thanked the flight attendant and was given the juice.

No matter how routine the situation, good manners are always good form.

Rule 14

TURN NOT YOUR BACK TO OTHERS, ESPECIALLY

IN SPEAKING. JOG [BUMP] NOT THE TABLE OR

DESK ON WHICH ANOTHER READS OR WRITES.

LEAN NOT UPON ANY ONE.

It's no coincidence that the expression "to turn one's back" has significance beyond the mere physical gesture. Establishing and maintaining eye contact is a sign of respect, politeness, and sincerity. Once you have begun a conversation, avoid being verbose. It's rude to monopolize another's time for the pleasure of hearing your own voice.

On the flip side, be an attentive listener. Never interrupt.

Be absolutely certain the speaker has finished before you begin. You may notice that all good talk show hosts and interviewers follow this rule. It does require patience to learn to hear someone out but it's what you would want for yourself. By listening patiently you can learn and you can figure out the solution.

Jogging is for the running track or the quiet trail or street. Walk carefully around the surfaces people are working on. What we are talking about here is physical leaning only. We all need someone we can lean on for help occasionally.

Rule 15

KEEP YOUR NAILS CLEAN AND SHORT, ALSO YOUR

HANDS AND TEETH CLEAN, YET WITHOUT SHEWING

[SHOWING] ANY GREAT CONCERN FOR THEM.

We need no translation—or signs on the inside of the restroom door—to remind us of the importance of cleanliness, which continues to be the mark of a civilized person. Concern in this area is a matter of health.

Do the necessary cleaning in private rather than in public. Nowadays, you do not have to spend much time on personal hygiene because of modern products and conveniences. Consistency is the key.

Rule 16

DO NOT PUFF UP THE CHEEKS, LOLL NOT OUT

THE TONGUE, RUB THE HANDS OR BEARD,

THRUST OUT THE LIPS OR BITE THEM, OR KEEP

THE LIPS TOO OPEN OR TOO CLOSE.

This rule applies to those who affect these physical expressions, particularly the sticking out of the tongue, unless in obvious jest. These practices show disrespect.

Do not criticize the imperfections of others. Since we all have some, it is best to overlook them.

Rule 17

BE NO FLATTERER; NEITHER PLAY WITH ANY THAT

DELIGHTS NOT TO BE PLAY'D WITHAL.

An age of sincerity and candor has dawned once again. People want straight talk, honesty, and openness.

Flattery has an element of exaggeration. A compliment or words of praise is one thing; flattery which smacks of manipulation is another. In time, most people see through flattery and begin to wonder what is behind the veil. Hyperbole should be avoided as well.

Eliminate the risk of being thought an opportunist. Speak plainly and without exaggeration, and avoid flattering or kissing up to those who find it a clear indication of insincerity. Also, kissing up diminishes a person's self-respect.

Do not tease others. While some might be good-humored about it, many will be hurt. Most people, children and adults alike, do not appreciate being taunted in this way. There is no point in risking the possibility of hurting someone's feelings or causing them anxiety.

Rule 18

READ NO LETTERS, BOOKS, OR PAPERS IN COMPANY, BUT WHEN THERE IS A NECESSITY FOR THE DOING OF IT YOU MUST LEAVE. COME NOT NEAR THE BOOKS OR WRITINGS OF ANOTHER SO AS TO READ THEM, UNLESS DESIRED, OR GIVE YOUR OPINION OF THEM UNASK'D. ALSO LOOK NOT NIGH WHEN ANOTHER IS WRITING A LETTER.

Respect and privacy—two sturdy threads of civility—are woven together in this rule. Do not read in the presence of others unless you are reading aloud to children or reading together. Respect the privacy of another's papers, messages, and work materials (including e-mails and texts) by not reading or commenting on them unless invited to.

A boss should not look over an employee's shoulder at a computer screen unless there is a good reason to do so. Similarly, employees should avert their eyes from the items on the desk of a manager or coworker.

Many people forget that those closest to them—their spouses and children—have a right to privacy as well. No one likes someone snooping around, no matter who it is.

If you need to check your e-mail or text messages or take a phone call, excuse yourself. When talking to someone individually or while in a group, do not constantly look at your phone. The occasional e-mail or text, however, can be glanced at, preferably during a lull in the conversation.

You might consider consecrating screen-free spaces or times. The Atlanta Hawks professional basketball team, for example, have team dinners where phones are disallowed in order to foster conversation.

Rule 19

LET YOUR COUNTENANCE BE PLEASANT BUT IN

SERIOUS MATTERS SOMEWHAT GRAVE.

This rule, too, refers to facial expressions, which might be considered mere window dressing, but there's depth to his message. People who broadcast a smile throughout the day create happiness within and without; they are on a positive spiral that pulls others in. Their laughter is contagious—and only humans can catch it. Your attitude is something other people can see.

William James, a prominent American psychologist, philosopher, and physician in the 1800s, said, "The greatest discovery of my generation is that a human being can alter his life by altering his attitude." Look for opportunities to spread cheer. Of course, there are times when gravity is appropriate. Know when a smile is not the best garb.

Letter to Marquis de Lafayette, August 15, 1786:

"HOWEVER UNIMPORTANT AMERICA

MAY BE CONSIDERED AT PRESENT,

AND HOWEVER BRITAIN MAY AFFECT

TO DESPISE HER TRADE, THERE WILL

ASSUREDLY COME A DAY, WHEN

THIS COUNTRY WILL HAVE SOME

WEIGHT IN THE SCALE OF EMPIRES."

G. Washington

Rule 20

THE GESTURES OF THE BODY MUST BE SUITED

TO THE DISCOURSE YOU ARE UPON.

As stated before, your body language should always be true to your purpose. If your nonverbal behavior does not match the verbal, you are being deceptive. Which will be believed?

Rule 21

REPROACH NONE FOR THE INFIRMITIES OF

NATURE, NOR DELIGHT TO PUT THEM THAT HAVE

IN MIND THEREOF.

Often we avoid making eye contact with disabled or elderly people. By not looking at them, we fail to acknowledge their existence. They become non-people.

We should all embrace the spirit of the Americans with Disabilities Act and treat those who are blind, deaf, in wheelchairs, or otherwise impaired with the same respect and acknowledgment we give others. They should be accommodated. The passage of the American with Disabilities Act nearly thirty years ago was a step in the right direction for our country but legislation is only the beginning. The way we act is what is crucial.

Friendly and helpful gestures are always appreciated. Kindness is a language that everyone, even the visually impaired, can see. It sends a message of respect from one human being to another. As Ellen DeGeneres always concludes her popular television show: "Be kind to one another."

Rule 22

SHEW NOT YOURSELF GLAD AT THE MISFORTUNE

OF ANOTHER, THOUGH HE WERE YOUR ENEMY.

Although "enemy" may be a strong word to describe our everyday rivals, it's nonetheless hard not to gloat when the convenience store clerk rejects the credit card of the man who just elbowed his way in front of you.

True civility requires that we fine-tune our sense of empathy and try to understand and find compassion for the people who have hurt us. It is far nobler to attempt to understand and accept the limitations of an unfriendly person than to stoop to that person's level by reciprocating. For some who are damaged by another, forgiveness is the key. For others, there can be no forgiveness for some acts. But even in situations where we can't forgive, protecting ourselves from self-destructive malice is best for our well-being.

Rule 23

WHEN YOU SEE A CRIME PUNISHED, YOU MAY BE

INWARDLY PLEASED, BUT ALWAYS SHEW PITY TO

THE SUFFERING OFFENDER.

This is a high standard of civility that is uncommon these days. We are more inclined to let it all hang out—we tend to show our inner feelings and reactions quite plainly in our demeanor and behavior, even when we know they are excessive or inappropriate. And how easy is it for us to pile on in the comments section when someone's being castigated online?

Rise to a higher level of conduct. Make the difficult separation between what you feel and what you know you should show. You must exercise restraint, but in some cases it is okay to be privately pleased if you believe justice has been done.

Rule 24

DO NOT LAUGH TOO LOUD OR TOO MUCH AT

ANY PUBLICK [SPECTACLE].

It is perfectly acceptable to laugh freely in private and in public as long as it is not at the expense of others. Laugh with, not at.

Rule 25

SUPERFLUOUS COMPLIMENTS AND ALL

AFFECTATION OF CEREMONIE ARE TO BE

AVOIDED, YET WHERE DUE THEY ARE NOT TO BE

NEGLECTED.

Here is another admonition against ingratiating and phony behavior. React with an appropriate portion of genuine admiration and do not pour on a sticky layer of goo just to get ahead and win favor.

Be true to yourself while you spare the feelings of others. Acknowledge events and accomplishments with the honor they deserve. One further note: Do not stand on ceremony. Your feet will hurt after a while. Break through!

George Washington was not a typical aristocrat. He was a man who liked to puncture pomposity. After he left the presidency, Washington preferred the title "general" to "president."

Rule 26

IN PULLING OFF YOUR HAT TO PERSONS OF

DISTINCTION, AS NOBLEMEN, JUSTICES,

CHURCHMEN, ETC., MAKE A REVERENCE,

BOWING MORE OR LESS ACCORDING TO THE

CUSTOM OF THE BETTER BRED AND QUALITY OF

THE PERSON. AMONGST YOUR EQUALS EXPECT

NOT ALWAYS THAT THEY SHOULD BEGIN WITH

YOU FIRST, BUT TO PULL OFF THE HAT WHEN

THERE IS NO NEED IS AFFECTATION. IN THE

MANNER OF SALUTING AND RESALUTING IN

WORDS, KEEP TO THE MOST USUAL CUSTOM.

We've put bowing and saluting behind us (except among the armed forces). Even today, patronizing gestures should be avoided. Shake all people's hands with a moderate grip and extend a healthy greeting.

As an expression of respect for our country, it is fitting to take off your hat when the colors are shown and the national anthem is played. Men should remove their hats in court.

Nowadays, it is okay to wear your hat indoors at the mall or at a casual restaurant, like a diner, pizzeria, or fast food place. Of course, it is more than okay to wear a baseball cap in an indoor arena or stadium or any outdoor venue.

Good manners dictate your hat should be removed when you are seated at a family meal at home, when you are a guest at someone's house, or when you are dining at a more formal restaurant. For men the hat should be off in church and at a funeral service. It is still nice for a man to remove his hat when meeting a lady. Aside from the aforementioned, common sense should be applied.

"IT APPEARS TO ME THAT LITTLE MORE

THAN COMMON SENSE AND COMMON

HONESTY, IN THE TRANSACTIONS

OF THE COMMUNITY AT LARGE,

WOULD BE NECESSARY TO MAKE

US A GREAT AND HAPPY NATION."

G. Washington

Rule 27

'TIS ILL MANNERS TO BID ONE MORE EMINENT
THAN YOURSELF BE COVERED, AS WELL AS NOT
TO DO IT TO WHOM IT'S DUE. LIKEWISE, HE THAT
MAKES TOO MUCH HASTE TO PUT ON HIS HAT
DOES NOT WELL. YET HE OUGHT TO PUT IT ON
AT THE FIRST, OR AT MOST THE SECOND TIME
OF BEING ASK'D. NOW WHAT IS HEREIN SPOKEN,
OF QUALIFICATION IN BEHAVIOUR IN SALUTING,
OUGHT ALSO TO BE OBSERVED IN TAKING OF
PLACE AND SITTING DOWN, FOR CEREMONIES
WITHOUT BOUNDS ARE TROUBLESOME.

How alien this all seems to us now! How mannered and irrelevant. True, we live in a (more or less) classless society.

If you discard the frilly language and transform the "one more eminent than yourself" into your professor, boss, manager, or the judge, this rule may suddenly take on a more modern look. It boils down to showing respect for your elders, teachers, supervisors, physicians, nurses, EMTs, public officials, and of course, everyone else. A wise person observes and respects the "ceremonies" that are meaningful to any who are present.

Rule 28

IF ANY ONE COME TO SPEAK TO YOU WHILE YOU

ARE SITTING, STAND UP, THOUGH HE BE YOUR

INFERIOR. AND WHEN YOU PRESENT SEATS, LET IT

BE TO EVERY ONE ACCORDING TO HIS DEGREE.

Class consciousness, which permeated the eighteenth century, manifested itself in many ways, including sitting and standing "according to degree." We no longer sit and stand on ceremony in this way. It is not necessary to join a person with whom we are conversing at that person's level unless it is awkward not to do so.

As a gesture of respect and deference, younger people ought to offer seats to older people on public transportation, the park bench, and wherever or whenever appropriate. Those acts convey a message that feels good for all parties.

Rule 29

WHEN YOU MEET WITH ONE OF GREATER

QUALITY THAN YOURSELF, STOP AND RETIRE,

ESPECIALLY IF IT BE AT A DOOR OR ANY STRAIGHT

PLACE, TO GIVE WAY FOR HIM TO PASS.

Although the basis of this rule—people of greater and lesser quality—is antiquated, we can still make good use of the principle by yielding to people in wheelchairs or on crutches, the elderly, and people with small children. Hold the door open for the sake of being polite. Do not be upset if not thanked. Doing good by being considerate is its own reward.

Concerning parking spaces, respect those marked for the disabled, expectant mothers, and parents with small children, as enlightened stores have designated.

Rule 30

IN WALKING, THE HIGHEST PLACE IN MOST

COUNTRYS SEEMS TO BE ON THE RIGHT HAND,

THEREFORE PLACE YOURSELF ON THE LEFT OF HIM

WHOM YOU DESIRE TO HONOUR. BUT IF THREE

WALK TOGETHER, THE MID[DLE] PLACE IS THE

MOST HONOURABLE. THE WALL IS USUALLY GIVEN

TO THE MOST WORTHY IF TWO WALK TOGETHER.

This musty practice was very important to those who hung out with royalty. Unless you do, you can ignore it and walk alongside your companion without concern as to right and left. The key is to be attentive to your walking mate.

Rule 31

IF ANY ONE FAR SURPASSES OTHERS EITHER

IN AGE, ESTATE, OR MERIT, [YET] WOULD GIVE

PLACE TO A MEANER [SOMEONE LOWER CLASS]

THAN HIMSELF, THE ONE OUGHT NOT TO

ACCEPT IT. SO HE ON THE OTHER PART SHOULD

NOT USE MUCH EARNESTNESS NOR OFFER IT

ABOVE ONCE OR TWICE.

According to this rule, someone of a lower class was to refuse the place offered by someone of greater age, wealth, or station. Nonsense. We have abandoned the idea of formal rank except in the military, police force, fire department, and airlines. A generous gesture by someone to someone else who is less fortunate should be lauded. It is an act of kindness to treat such a person with empathy.

Learning from the Best

When I was a rookie lawyer, I had the good fortune of being invited to the office of Mr. Murdoch, a well-established and highly respected real estate attorney and a prominent member of the local bar association. The event was an estate closing, in which a house was to change hands.

Being new to the profession and aware of this man's reputation and seniority, I felt nervous and intimidated as I entered his staid, old law office. While we shook hands, I thanked him for allowing me to observe.

Mr. Murdoch immediately took me into the conference room and introduced me to the buyers and sellers as a young attorney who would like to observe the closing. Before I arrived, he had asked if anyone had an objection. No one did.

Then, looking at me over his half-glasses, he asked if I would like a cup of coffee. I said I would, if it was not too much trouble. With that, he walked to a side room and returned with a cup, which he handed to me. Mr. Murdoch did not ask a secretary, law clerk, or legal assistant to serve me, although it would've certainly been all right to do so.

Even before the legal proceedings began, I learned from this important and gracious man to treat juniors with grace and to ensure that newcomers are made to feel comfortable in a potentially awkward situation.

It is important at the doctor's or dentist's office, lawyer's office, or any office in general, for the receptionist to be welcoming both on the telephone and at the office. You deserve an attentive and pleasant reception by all such people you encounter. The professionalism of the staff, for the most part, is a reflection of the professional you are seeing.

Rule 32

TO ONE THAT IS YOUR EQUAL OR NOT MUCH

INFERIOR, YOU ARE TO GIVE THE CHIEF PLACE

IN YOUR LODGING. AND HE TO WHOM 'TIS

OFFERED OUGHT AT THE FIRST TO REFUSE IT

BUT AT THE SECOND TO ACCEPT, THOUGH

NOT WITHOUT ACKNOWLEDGING HIS OWN

UNWORTHINESS.

A generous spirit of hospitality is one of the hallmarks of a civil society. Offer the best to your guest. Sometimes it is necessary to offer twice or insist upon it, especially when someone says they don't want to put you out. And as guests, we should be willing to accept the kindness of others. The important thing is to be mutually welcoming when it comes to hospitable offers.

Learning to Accept

Many people spend a great deal of time living in accordance with the adage that "it is better to give than to receive." So much so that they may end up never being able to comfortably receive.

It is important to both give and receive graciously. When you accept something, regardless of what you think of it, you must act pleased. That makes the person who has given it feel good. When you give, you derive pleasure from the recipient's joy. And remember that giving during the holiday season may or may not be reciprocal, depending upon the nature of the relationship.

Rule 33

THEY THAT ARE IN DIGNITY OR IN OFFICE HAVE IN

ALL PLACES PRECEDENCY, BUT WHILST THEY ARE

YOUNG THEY OUGHT TO RESPECT THOSE THAT

ARE THEIR EQUALS IN BIRTH OR OTHER QUALITYS,

THOUGH THEY HAVE NO PUBLICK CHARGE.

Yield is a good sign for many intersections on the road of life. Develop the habit of holding the door open, stopping to let others pass, allowing others to speak first if you both start together, and excusing yourself if you bump into someone. And those who yield to you ought to be audibly thanked. Of course, all people should be treated the same no matter what.

The Highway Commuter

Yolanda commuted by car from her home in the suburbs to the city. The highway was always crowded, and the heavy traffic crept along bumper-to-bumper. Even on days she started out early, she barely arrived on time.

On one particular morning in the middle of an exhausting week, Yolanda left home with her headlights on since it was not quite light outside. Some of the early commuters had no lights on, which she found inconsiderate and dangerous.

Yolanda had to aggressively force her way onto the busy highway because no one would slow down to safely let her enter from the on-ramp even though she used her signal. Once on the highway, though, Yolanda was a courteous driver. She allowed others to enter the road by yielding. She let people who needed to change lanes do so ahead of her. She did not tailgate, and she always signaled early when she was about to change lanes.

All of this cost her nothing. Some of the drivers returned the favor. Some waved in her direction in appreciation as they passed. Yolanda was pleased with that gesture. She was glad to see others acting responsibly by being considerate.

We are all on the highway together. We should communicate effectively with reciprocal courtesy. The result is a safer, less stressful, and more pleasant trip.

Rule 34

IT IS GOOD MANNERS TO PREFER THEM

TO WHOM WE SPEAK BEFORE OURSELVES,

ESPECIALLY IF THEY BE ABOVE US, WITH WHOM

IN NO SORT WE OUGHT TO BEGIN.

Above or below has no bearing today. But if we have good manners, we graciously let others speak first. We let them finish without interruption. We permit them their point of view. It isn't always necessary to contradict or force a confrontation if you disagree with someone.

From a Letter to John Sullivan, May 11, 1781:

"IT IS MUCH EASIER TO AVOID

DISAGREEMENTS THAN TO

REMOVE DISCONTENTS."

G Washington

Rule 35

LET YOUR DISCOURSE WITH MEN OF BUSINESS

BE SHORT AND COMPREHENSIVE.

As noted in the introduction, please bear in mind that 250 years ago all generic pronouns and nouns were in the masculine. Of course, the rules should now be considered gender neutral.

This rule is even more relevant today because we have less time. It's true that most of us may live longer but we have less unscheduled time in each day. So strive for concision in your voice mail messages, e-mails, social media posts, and texts. Be short and to the point in business communication, which depends on a delicate balance between substance and brevity. When you make a presentation, know your material so well you can boil it down to its essence. It is inconsiderate to waste the time of others.

And don't frivolously extend group discussions. Disagree or question only when important—and not just because you haven't been heard at a particular meeting and want the boss to know you're there. Abraham Lincoln put it this way: "Better to remain silent and be thought a fool than to speak and remove all doubt."

George Washington's
second inaugural address,
given in Philadelphia,
was the shortest one ever.
It was only 135 words.

Rule 36

ARTIFICERS [TRICKSTERS] AND PERSONS OF

LOW DEGREE OUGHT NOT TO USE MANY

CEREMONIES TO LORDS OR OTHERS OF HIGH

DEGREE, BUT RESPECT AND HIGHLY HONOR

THEM, AND THOSE OF HIGH DEGREE OUGHT TO

TREAT THEM WITH AFFABILITY AND COURTESIE,

WITHOUT ARROGANCY.

When we examine this rule through a modern monocle that screens out references to tricksters and persons of low and high degree, we see advice we can relate to our daily lives. Regardless of the station of the people we come in contact with, look for the common denominator and respond accordingly. There is always common ground.

Behave naturally, respecting everyone you report to and those who report to you. Ingratiating and fawning behavior sounds a sour note when we are conducting business and engaging in social activities.

An attitude of arrogance curdles the air between us. No matter how much you achieve, do not assume a cloak of superiority; remain human and humble.

Rule 37

IN SPEAKING TO MEN OF QUALITY, DO NOT
LEAN NOR LOOK THEM FULL IN THE FACE, NOR
APPROACH TOO NEAR THEM. AT LEAST KEEP A
FULL PACE FROM THEM.

Then and now we all need our space. It can be annoying, intimidating, or even threatening to have someone edge up too close to you. Many of us intentionally or unintentionally invade the space of others.

A gentle reminder: different people have different levels of comfort with physical familiarity. Try to tune in and err on the side of respectful distance. Remember that norms around personal space also vary by country and culture.

Further regarding social norms, it is good manners to establish appropriate eye contact when speaking to someone. Do not be "in their face."

At the Bank

Fred was in line at the bank. When his turn came, he waved hello to Ms. Williams, a friendly teller he had known for years. She was at the next window over.

The woman next in line went to Ms. Williams's window and handed her a check to be cashed. Ms. Williams politely explained that it was bank policy not to cash checks for people who did not have an account there. In these instances, she explained in a professional manner, proper identification and a fingerprint were necessary. Upon hearing this, the woman exploded in a series of profanities, berating both the teller and the bank.

Ms. Williams politely went over the policy once again and was treated to another outburst of expletives. This profane attack caused Ms. Williams to begin to quietly cry.

Appalled by this woman's conduct, Fred turned to her and told her she was being very rude to Ms. Williams. The woman gave Fred a surprised look and told him to mind his own damn business. When Fred apologized to Ms. Williams on the woman's behalf, the woman angrily told her not to accept the apology.

Just then the bank manager, who saw and heard from her office that there was a fuss, came over and asked the woman to leave immediately. Later, Fred was told that the manager barred her from ever returning.

When Fred reflected on this incident, it occurred to him that someone—or everyone—in the line who was within hearing distance should have stepped forward to verbally back him up in this safe setting. Security was present.

The word must go out that uncivilized behavior will not be tolerated. If more of us stand up for what is right in a safe setting, there will be tremendous social pressure on others to behave properly. Call it the "civility defense squad."

Another important aspect to be addressed is the woman's anger. It is important to note that anger is a universal emotion. Everyone gets angry at times. What is important is what you do with your anger. You must pay attention to how you speak and act when you get angry. "When angry," Thomas Jefferson said, "count ten before you speak; if very angry, a hundred."

Rule 38

IN VISITING THE SICK, DO NOT PRESENTLY

PLAY THE PHYSICIAN IF YOU BE NOT KNOWING

THEREIN.

Don't misrepresent yourself when offering advice—especially medical advice. It is relatively easy to get good information and treatment today. EMTs, physician assistants, nurse practitioners, and registered nurses under the auspices of a physician can provide that advice and render some medical treatment.

Generally speaking, if you are asked to provide guidance in an area in which you are not well versed, couch your response in terms that make clear you are a novice: "I'm not an expert, but . . ."

In a broader sense, act with honesty and candor. Don't fake it. Here's a tip: three little words that are among the most difficult to say are also the most freeing. Are you ready? Here they are: "I don't know." These words may be followed by, when appropriate, "but I'll find someone who does know."

Rule 39

IN WRITING OR SPEAKING, GIVE TO EVERY
PERSON HIS DUE TITLE ACCORDING TO HIS
DEGREE AND THE CUSTOM OF THE PLACE.

We no longer concern ourselves with "due titles" such as King, Queen, Prince, Princess, Count, Duchess, or Marquis. These titles were usually inherited and did, back then, play an important role in one's social standing. And those titles were frequently invoked because formalities of writing and speech were carefully observed.

Much of that formality has disappeared from our social surroundings, and we tend to be more casual in our modes of address, both written and spoken. Nevertheless, the fact is that some people bear titles that have been earned by their academic efforts or vocation, such as officeholders, physicians, judges, and religious leaders. In those cases it is proper to give the appropriate acknowledgment.

Rule 40

STRIVE NOT WITH YOUR SUPERIORS IN ARGUMENT,

BUT ALWAYS SUBMIT YOUR JUDGMENT TO OTHERS

WITH MODESTY.

Be careful, be circumspect, be civil. If you disagree, don't argue defensively. Listen carefully to what is being said, and then respond as vigorously as you wish—but with diplomatic restraint and respectful consideration.

Using soft language, such as "it seems to me" or "it might be that" or "help me understand," shows that you recognize other views are feasible. And consider this: always focus your attention on the issues being discussed and not on the person doing the discussing. When you find yourself judging the person, that's the time to stop talking, take a breath, and regroup.

Rule 41

UNDERTAKE NOT TO TEACH YOUR EQUAL IN

THE ART HE HIMSELF PROFESSES; IT SAVOURS OF

ARROGANCY.

As stated earlier, make sure to resist the urge to give advice to a peer unless requested to do so. Listen carefully when you think your advice is being sought; you may be mistaken.

Arrogance serves no purpose in this or any other situation. True self-confidence engenders respect for self and others whereas arrogance sets up a power play. Find the balance between confidence and arrogance. Feel good about yourself but keep your ego in check. It is always best to be humble and self-deprecating.

Letter to Benjamin Franklin, October 18, 1782:

"I AM MUCH OBLIGED BY THE

POLITICAL INFORMATION WHICH

YOU HAVE TAKEN THE TROUBLE TO

CONVEY TO ME, BUT FEEL MYSELF

MUCH EMBARRASSED IN MY WISH

TO MAKE YOU A RETURN IN KIND."

G. Washington

Rule 42

LET THY CEREMONIES IN COURTESIE BE PROPER

TO THE DIGNITY OF HIS PLACE WITH WHOM YOU

CONVERSE, FOR IT IS ABSURD TO ACT THE SAME

WITH A CLOWN AND A PRINCE.

In colonial society, firm distinctions were made between a "clown" (which meant a country bumpkin) and a prince (which meant a lot more than a prince of a fellow). Much has changed.

We are all connected. We should be courteous in our diverse society, respecting the dignity of all those with whom we converse and have dealings with. It is helpful to have meaningful contact with persons of all ages, ethnicities, countries of national origin, and genders. In that way you gain perspective. Treat all equally well. The strength of our country comes from diversity. Our belief in a civil society is based on consideration, empathy, sensitivity, kindness, and tolerance.

Judging People

The following story is more folktale than history—but stirring nonetheless.

A woman in a faded gingham dress and her husband, dressed in a homespun, threadbare suit, stepped off the train in Boston and walked timidly, without an appointment, into the Harvard University president's outer office. The secretary could tell in a moment that such backwoods country hicks had no business at Harvard and probably didn't even deserve to be in Cambridge. She frowned.

"We want to see the president," the man said softly. "He'll be busy all day," the secretary snapped. "We'll wait," the woman replied.

For hours the secretary ignored them, hoping the couple would become discouraged and go away. When they didn't, the secretary grew frustrated and finally decided to disturb the president, even though it was a chore she always regretted.

"Maybe if they just see you for a few minutes, they'll leave," she told him. He sighed in exasperation and nodded. Someone of his importance obviously didn't have the time to spend with them. Furthermore, he detested gingham dresses and homespun suits cluttering up his outer office. Stern-faced, nose up in the air, the president strutted toward the couple.

The woman told him, "We had a son who attended Harvard for one year. He loved Harvard. He was happy here. But about a year ago he was accidentally killed. My husband and I would like to erect a memorial to him, somewhere on campus."

The president wasn't touched; he was shocked. "Madam," he said gruffly and in a condescending way, "we can't put up a statue for every person who attended Harvard and died. If we did, this place would look like a cemetery."

"Oh, no," the woman explained quickly. "We don't want to erect a statue. We thought we would like to give a building to Harvard."

The president rolled his eyes. He glanced at the gingham dress and homespun suit and then exclaimed, "Building! Do you have any earthly idea how much a building costs? We have over seven and a half million dollars in the physical plant at Harvard."

For a moment the woman was silent. The president was pleased. He could get rid of them now. Then she turned to her husband and said quietly, "Is that all it costs to build a university? Why don't we just start our own?"

Her husband nodded. The president's face wilted in confusion and bewilderment. Mr. and Mrs. Leland Stanford walked out and went to Palo Alto, California, where they established the university that bears their name as a memorial to a son that Harvard no longer cared about.

You can judge the character of others by how they treat those they think can do nothing for them or to them.

Although he founded a great university, George Washington never went to college. He had the least schooling of any of the Founding Fathers, most of whom had gone to university in Great Britain. Although he did not have the benefit of higher education, he loved to read and learn.

Rule 43

DO NOT EXPRESS JOY BEFORE ONE SICK OR

IN PAIN, FOR THAT CONTRARY PASSION WILL

AGGRAVATE HIS MISERY.

The key to so many interpersonal situations, including this one, is empathy. Turn on your wide bandwidth and tune all your senses to the ill person's signals. How will your broadcast be received? Will your efforts to uplift a flagging spirit be heard? How much joviality is appropriate? Then moderate your mood and your message of sympathy to the proper volume and stay only as long as you are welcome.

Be sure to check on friends and relatives who have been ill and be willing to supply what is needed if they are unable to provide for themselves. The hospital room is often a cheerless, impersonal place. Visitors can break up the endless day and bring cheer, but they should not overstay their visits. Several short visits will bring more healing than one interminable one.

This rule also applies when writing to someone over social media. Be careful when you write a message of sympathy on

Facebook, for example, that you are not sharing information that the ill person prefers to be kept private. In fact, be careful about opening up your world using Facebook.

At Peace

Bill's friend, Rick, had terminal cancer. And Rick's wife, Sally, was doing all she could for him in his final months.

One of Rick's pleasures in life was boating. He had often motored in his small boat on a beautiful lake near his home. When he became ill, however, he had to sell it.

Sally called Bill's wife, Ruth, and a day on the lake on Bill's boat was arranged. The couples got together on a perfect spring day. Rick, pale and thin, enjoyed himself as they floated leisurely on the water, soaking up the sun and the scenery. At the end of the day, Rick and Sally hugged and thanked Bill and Ruth.

A week later, Bill visited Rick at his home. They talked about the lake, fishing, boats, and of the lovely day they had spent together. Ten days later, Bill died. A few days after the funeral, Sally called Bill to thank him again for the day on the lake and for not discussing Rick's illness during his visit. Bill replied that Rick did not bring it up so neither did he.

Generosity and empathy, two attributes of civility Bill and Sally showed toward their dying friend, are always appreciated. It is all about human kindness.

Rule 44

WHEN A MAN DOES ALL HE CAN, THOUGH IT

SUCCEEDS NOT WELL, BLAME NOT HIM THAT DID IT.

Commendation—not criticism—is called for when one makes a good effort. Blame is like rubbing salt in the wound of a person who has labored unsuccessfully. Failure is its own punishment—but can often lead to later success. A friend offers a gentle word of empathy and a boost to the deflated spirit.

A good-faith attempt and persistence in the face of failure are the first steps on the road to success. After winning one term in the U.S. House of Representatives, Abraham Lincoln lost his bid for reelection. Six years later, he lost yet another election when he ran for the United States Senate. He persisted. Five years later, in 1860, he was elected the sixteenth president of the United States of America.

Although this rule is pertinent to many occasions, it is particularly applicable to sporting events. Persistence is the key, but when your team loses, never point a finger at one player who no doubt has already taken on a large share of the blame. Shared accountability is at the core of what it means to be a team.

Members of that team must relate to each other in a positive way, overlooking error and celebrating success.

Children are particularly prone to believe they are responsible for a team's failures. It's important to cite their efforts and those of their teammates. Blame no one in particular. The important thing is to try your best and have fun while exercising good sportsmanship.

Rule 45

BEING TO ADVISE OR REPREHEND ANY ONE,

CONSIDER WHETHER IT OUGHT TO BE IN

PUBLICK OR IN PRIVATE, PRESENTLY OR AT SOME

OTHER TIME, IN WHAT TERMS TO DO IT, AND IN

REPROVING SHEW [SHOW] NO SIGN OF CHOLAR

[ANGER], BUT DO IT WITH ALL SWEETNESS AND

MILDNESS.

People who are being criticized constructively listen better when the language is soft, the tone is quiet, and the setting is private. There is nothing more humiliating than a loud, public reprimand. Discreet, constructive criticism can push a person in the right direction.

Never reprimand over social media such as Facebook, Twitter, or Instagram. Use caution in using the "cc" and "bcc" lines in your e-mail. No matter how justified, destructive public criticism always hurts the person criticizing more than the recipient. It is cruel. It is human nature to feel sympathy for the one being berated.

This advice is especially useful for parents. Some of us who would never think to publicly reprimand an adult do so without a thought when a child misbehaves. A child can be just as humiliated as an adult. Take the time and the energy to remove the child from the situation and talk quietly about the inappropriate behavior. You will be giving your child respect as well as discipline.

You will be setting an example of civilized parenting.

Constructive Criticism

I felt my knees knocking that day in court. It was my first jury trial and I was very nervous. Judge John McAuliffe, known to be brilliant and thorough, was presiding. The trial was over in the afternoon, and the jury returned a verdict in our favor.

Emboldened by my success, I approached the judge and told him the trial was my very first. He immediately responded from the bench that it didn't show. I thanked him for that gracious remark.

This same judge took me aside at a bar association meeting a few days later and told me that I might be a little less long-winded next time I spoke to a jury. I thanked him again.

Rule 46

TAKE ALL ADMONITIONS THANKFULLY IN

WHAT TIME OR PLACE SOEVER GIVEN, BUT

AFTERWARDS, NOT BEING CULPABLE, TAKE A

TIME AND PLACE CONVENIENT TO LET HIM

KNOW IT THAT GAVE THEM.

Be sure to thank a person for warning you of some condition that threatens you. That person is being empathetic. If you do not look out for others, you are someone who thinks the world revolves around you.

This selfish attitude will cause you to mistreat others even if unintended. Dwelling on yourself will deny you the opportunity to enjoy others and they you.

Rule 47

MOCK NOT NOR JEST AT ANY THING OF IMPORTANCE, BREAK NO JESTS THAT ARE SHARP AND BITING, AND IF YOU DELIVER ANY THING WITTY AND PLEASANT, ABSTAIN FROM LAUGHING THEREAT YOURSELF.

Again, never joke at anything that is of serious importance. Your words could easily be misinterpreted, especially online—without context or physical and verbal cues. Be careful in using comic relief.

Avoid laughing at your own jokes—it's not flattering. If you can't help it, at the very least be sure you are not the only person doing so.

On the other hand, learn to laugh at yourself. In fact, laugh at yourself before anyone else can. Others enjoy self-deprecating humor. And it also keeps your ego in check.

Rule 48

WHEREIN YOU REPROVE ANOTHER BE

UNBLAMABLE YOURSELF, FOR EXAMPLE IS MORE

PREVALENT THAN PRECEPTS.

You've no doubt heard these two ideas before: "Let him that is without sin cast the first stone," and "Actions speak louder than words." These adages can be woven together for a doubly potent bit of advice to remind us to look to our own behavior before that of others.

Here's another way of expressing the first concept: "Don't attempt to remove a speck from your brother's eye when there is a log in your own." Most of us see the shortcomings of others as much bigger than our own, if we see ours at all. Turn the magnifying glass around and scrutinize your behavior before decrying that of others.

The second adage encourages us to lead by example. Civil people refrain from casting blame. They are more inclined to try to excuse the uncivil behavior of others by attributing it to some temporary factor, such as confusion, ill health, or fatigue rather than malevolence or selfishness.

This double-duty rule is worthy of a great deal of consideration. Try to incorporate it into your everyday activities and note the results.

Road Rage

There seems to be only one place we encounter incivility more than politics these days: highways. More and more people drive on roads that were not meant to carry the current load. This causes traffic conditions to get worse and worse. Drivers become frustrated by delays due to accidents, and tempers flare.

We ought to be extending courtesies to those who share the road with us. Why not let someone who is signaling get into your lane? A wave should acknowledge thanks. You would take the time and expend the effort to hold a door open for someone entering a building. Maybe we all need to let go of the self-centered attitude that seems to take over when some of us get behind the wheel.

Safety is paramount. If you witness an aggressive driver on the road and have other than a hand-held phone in your car, you can do something about the menace. Virtually all states have made stopping aggressive drivers a priority. Signs on many highways give a phone number you can call to report a dangerous driver. Do not go after the aggressive driver yourself. In fact, never take things into your own hands when you are upset with the way others are driving. Be patient and tolerant. Turn on your favorite news station or play some music.

Suspected drunk drivers should certainly be reported as soon as possible. Calling the police is a better solution than countering with your own aggression, which may be dangerous for you and for those in your car—as well as for others who happen to be traveling on the same road. Just stay away, for safety's sake.

Take a stand by always being in control, being considerate, and exercising caution while driving on the roadways. Drive carefully as if your life, the lives of your passengers, and the lives of those sharing the roads depended on it—because they do.

Rule 49

USE NO REPROACHFUL LANGUAGE AGAINST ANY

ONE. NEITHER CURSE NOR REVILE.

You are alone in the house attending to chores and making repairs. Suddenly you drop the hammer squarely on your small toe. Your yelp of pain is followed by a string of loud swear words and curses. In that circumstance, it's difficult for even the most civil of us to contain an explosion of profanity. But otherwise, we would be much better off curbing our tongues.

When it is directed angrily at another person, profanity demeans us—not those against whom we use it. And it usually backfires. Those on the receiving end in turn react angrily and defensively. The use of expletives in argument weakens the speaker's case.

In any situation, but especially in professional or business settings, restrain your raw and indelicate tongue. The use of vulgarity and profanity is not substantive and does not convey strength. Lower the volume. Speak with purpose and force if necessary but omit the vulgarities.

What is stated in the rule is the gold standard. Profanity has come to be common, even acceptable, in contemporary culture.

The use of profanity does not mean someone is not a good person. Many decent people use expletives. In fact, our society is becoming immune to profanity due to its prevalence. That is not a good thing, but it is real.

Sometimes mixing language with expletives becomes a habit even with civil people. They think nothing of using it. They believe it is impactful but the message is often lost when surrounded by profane words. But habits can be broken. "Friggin'" is a good substitute. It can be difficult to find substitutes for other common four-letter words but get creative. It simply takes commitment to change after becoming aware of the behavior.

In many households, profane words are said in the presence of children. Needless to say, this does not set a good example, normalizing their use. Hopefully, the parents realize what they are doing and cease doing it. Habitual swearing may easily be passed on to the young ones, which can hamper them down the road.

Losing the Argument

It is said that George Washington was sitting at the dinner table one evening with some of his relatives, enjoying a good conversation. Suddenly, one of the men started to argue a point with one of the others. Every other word he used was profane. Washington immediately turned to him and remarked that he must have a very weak argument if he needed to rely on profanity instead of words of substance to sway his opponent.

Rule 50

BE NOT HASTY TO BELIEVE FLYING REPORTS TO THE DISPARAGEMENT OF ANY.

Although tabloids like *Star* and the *National Enquirer* didn't exist 250 years ago, rumors and disparaging reports proliferated almost to the extent that they do today. Nowadays, we are bombarded with hearsay in print, on television, and through social media. So much "news" is coming from unknown and questionable sources. It is imperative that you go to the most true and time-honored sources available.

In these days of prevalent social media, rumormongering and seeking out bad news about public figures, including celebrities, is very common. Some websites and blogs specialize in this content. But instead of focusing on the negative things in other people's lives, focus on the positive things in your own life.

Now, as then, "flying reports" ought to fall on deaf ears and should certainly not be given additional lift. Ignore gossip and rumors. Squelch them if you can by going to the source to get accurate information. Never launch a false or unsubstantiated story.

On a related note, cyberbullying has become a serious problem today, much more serious than many adults realize. Like traditional bullying, it damages a child's confidence and self-esteem. Unfortunately, a child is constantly within reach of a cyberbully through a text, social media post, or online video. And the problem is compounded because these taunts are open to a large audience. It is more crucial than ever for parents to build up the self-confidence of their children as a way to preempt and mitigate this behavior.

Parents should talk to their children about cyberbullying—teaching them how to respond as a bystander, helping process emotions if they've been a victim, and stressing the consequences of their actions if they've been a bully. In order to raise a generation of civil people, parents have a duty to familiarize themselves with the tools of social media and help their children navigate through an ever-changing world.

Rule 51

WEAR NOT YOUR CLOTHS FOUL, RIPT, OR DUSTY,

BUT SEE THEY BE BRUSH'D ONCE EVERY DAY AT

LEAST AND TAKE HEED THAT YOU APPROACH

NOT TO ANY UNCLEANNESS.

Preteens, teens, and young adults are pretty much exempt from this rule. Ripped, well-worn clothes and grimy but lucky hats are badges of belonging for these age groups.

Of course, clothes are not as important as the person who wears them. Comfortable clothes are nice, but all of us must always be presentable for the occasion. Remember that you show respect by being appropriately attired.

For the rest of us, clean, intact clothing is always required. It was a lot harder to do this back in colonial times. The clothing was much fussier than today and washing machines and dryers were yet to be invented. There were no dry cleaners. So enjoy the luxury of our modern methods and the wonderful smell and feel of well-washed garments. Heaven forbid a hat being washed.

Rule 52

IN YOUR APPAREL BE MODEST AND ENDEAVOR

TO ACCOMMODATE NATURE, RATHER THAN TO

PROCURE ADMIRATION. KEEP TO THE FASHION

OF YOUR EQUALS, SUCH AS ARE CIVIL AND

ORDERLY WITH RESPECT TO TIMES AND PLACES.

Many of us prefer the natural look to the glamorous one. As previously stated, clothes are not nearly as important as the person who dons them.

There are some who subscribe to the anything-goes and the more-outrageous-the-better school of dressing. Although in the minority, they are often in the public eye, taking advantage of this era of more personal freedom. They seek attention, which is basically okay as long as it is not too extreme. In show business it is all right to be showy but not tasteless. If you work or spend most of your time at home, obviously this isn't an issue.

Halloween is, of course, exempt. In fact, a costume is expected. The Christmas spirit compels some to adorn themselves accordingly. It is all in keeping with the spirit of the holidays.

In summary, if you remember that what you wear sends a message and you choose clothes that are appropriate for the occasion, you won't ever be out of style.

Rule 53

RUN NOT IN THE STREETS, NEITHER GO TOO
SLOWLY NOR WITH MOUTH OPEN. GO NOT
SHAKING YOUR ARMS, KICK NOT THE EARTH
WITH YOUR FEET, GO NOT UPON THE TOES NOR
IN A DANCING FASHION.

In the eighteenth century, physical activity in the streets was much more regulated. Today, we delight in seeing children and adults on bicycles (or even skateboards), neighbors out jogging or walking, parents pushing carriages, pet owners walking dogs, and postal service workers delivering mail and packages. These people help make our neighborhoods lively and festive.

Block parties, open-house parties, Halloween and Fourth of July festivities, holiday parades, town hall meetings, and farmers' markets help restore a sense of community so often lost in large cities and suburbs.

Rule 54

PLAY NOT THE PEACOCK, LOOKING EVERY

WHERE ABOUT TO SEE IF YOU BE WELL DECK'T, IF

YOUR SHOES FIT WELL, IF YOUR STOCKINGS SIT

NEATLY AND CLOTHES HANDSOMELY.

Vanity is an unbecoming trait that smacks of self-absorption. It is aligned with conceit. It is all about the "me" mentality.

Pay heed to the condition of your clothes and check that all buttons are buttoned and all zippers zipped, but keep track of how much time you're spending in front of the mirror.

"DO NOT CONCEIVE THAT FINE CLOTHES MAKE FINE MEN, ANY MORE THAN FINE FEATHERS MAKE FINE BIRDS. A PLAIN, GENTEEL DRESS IS MORE ADMIRED AND OBTAINS MORE CREDIT THAN LACE AND EMBROIDERY IN THE EYES OF THE JUDICIOUS AND SENSIBLE."

G. Washington

Rule 55

EAT NOT IN THE STREETS NOR IN THE HOUSE,

OUT OF SEASON.

Eating meals at regular intervals, whether at home or not, is still a sound practice. It is unclear what was meant by "out of season."

Rule 56

ASSOCIATE YOURSELF WITH MEN OF

GOOD QUALITY IF YOU ESTEEM YOUR OWN

REPUTATION; FOR 'TIS BETTER TO BE ALONE

THAN IN BAD COMPANY.

A couple of truisms apply here: (1) you are judged by the company you keep, and (2) if you lie down with dogs, you rise up with fleas.

Associate yourself with people who are truly civil: honest, truthful, caring, loyal, trustworthy, and empathetic. Be a person who can be counted on, and count on people like yourself. Remember, even the list of "friends" you have on social media can be considered the company you keep and are available for all to see.

Rule 57

IN WALKING UP AND DOWN IN A HOUSE, WITH

ONLY ONE IN COMPANY, IF HE BE GREATER THAN

YOURSELF, AT THE FIRST GIVE HIM THE RIGHT HAND

AND STOP NOT TILL HE DOES AND BE NOT THE

FIRST THAT TURNS, AND WHEN YOU DO LET IT BE

WITH YOUR FACE TOWARDS HIM. IF HE BE A MAN

OF GREAT QUALITY, WALK NOT WITH HIM CHEEK BY

JOWL BUT SOMEWHAT BEHIND, BUT YET IN SUCH A

MANNER THAT HE MAY EASILY SPEAK TO YOU.

Okay, I'm stumped. This is a totally antiquated rule with no modern application.

Rule 58

LET YOUR CONVERSATION BE WITHOUT MALICE OR ENVY, FOR 'TIS A SIGN OF A TRACTABLE AND COMMENDABLE NATURE. AND IN ALL CAUSES OF PASSION, ADMIT REASON TO GOVERN.

Spare others from words tinged by envy and malice even when you find yourself in the company of those who flaunt their riches and accomplishments. Display a commendable nature. Earn the respect of others by avoiding words of jealousy. Live your own life without ill-will or envy toward others and you will live longer and be happier.

On the flip side of this coin, be willing to praise others for their accomplishments while feeling inwardly secure whether or not you are acknowledged for your accomplishments and good deeds. Doing good is its own reward.

A SHORT TALE OF CIVILITY
Controlling Anger

I am guilty of not controlling my anger at times. But no matter how difficult, anger must be managed.

I was invited to be the "table talker" on the subject of civility one night at a group that meets at a restaurant. The people in the group are united in their efforts to help the community and generally try to bring about people treating each other with greater respect so that things will be better.

As I was beginning to speak about George Washington's rules from my seat at the table of twelve, a man sitting across the table interrupted me. He said words to the effect that Washington was a dishonest landowner who committed fraud to cheat people in order to obtain land.

I was angry and did not hold back as I should. I lost my cool by loudly dressing down this man for interrupting my presentation and disparaging the "father of our country." While I was speaking about the importance of civility, I was being uncivil at that moment.

My heart was racing. I could feel my blood pressure soaring. It took me several moments and a few deep breaths to calm down. Then, realizing how I reacted in this situation, I apologized to the man and everyone present.

After my presentation was over, I approached the man to apologize again. He accepted my apology. We shook hands and it was over.

Rule 59

NEVER EXPRESS ANYTHING UNBECOMING NOR

ACT AGAINST THE RULES MORAL BEFORE YOUR

INFERIOURS.

The civil boss should not be bossy, arrogant, or condescending. He or she should be humbled by their position and power. In the world of office power politics, managers who treat those who work for them with respect and decency are, in turn, respected and admired. There is never any reason to look down upon another.

Hold fast to your moral standards in the workplace and watch them suffuse those who work with you. Your moral tone will have wide-reaching effects. Morale is high when the culture is one of encompassing respect. So is retention of employees.

It is vital to establish a good reputation. There is no substitute for it. To quote another one of our great framers, Benjamin Franklin, "Glass, china, and reputation are easily cracked and never mended well."

When chosen commander in chief of the American forces, George Washington wrote of the "extensive and important trust" he felt had been bestowed upon him. This was an expression of his abiding humility and strong moral character. All of his life he held fast to his moral standards—no matter what.

OF CIVILITY

Among the many teachers who played an important role in my life, none compares to the late Joe Black, the former Brooklyn Dodgers pitcher who was my public school teacher and baseball coach after his Major League career was over. Mr. Black's conduct as a teacher, a mentor, and a civil person of principle greatly influenced me.

In 2010, eight years after his death, I wrote a biography of this universally respected man, *Meet the Real Joe Black*. In researching his life, I gained an insight into how he developed his strong moral character and parallel virtue of civility. What follows is a brief, and hopefully illuminating, summary of his life.

JOE BLACK grew up in a close-knit, but poor, family that included his mother, father, and five siblings. They lived in a small, modest house in an African American neighborhood of Plainfield, New Jersey. His mother, Martha Black, gave daily chore assignments, which Joe would later say were their early introduction to responsibility.

The Black household was located next to my father's auto body shop. When leaving the shop to go home, my father would see young Joe throwing rocks against the concrete front stoop of his house every day. One day when they were waving to each other, my father approached Joe. He tossed a white sphere into the air. Joe caught it and stared at it for a moment. It was the first baseball he ever touched. Joe looked up to thank my father, but it was too late—Nathan Selzer was down the road.

Joe was an excellent student but in high school he was routinely placed in the industrial arts track with all the other young black men. The black women were all put in the home economics program. The backward and racist school policy was that these classes would better prepare them for the work world.

When she found out, Martha Black wasn't having any of it. The very next day she went with Joe to see the principal, saying, "Don't you tell me how poor we are or what's gonna happen to my children. Joe is going to go to college." The principal flushed but recognized she meant business. Joe was immediately transferred to another track that included college preparatory classes.

He became the first in his family to continue education beyond high school, at Morgan State College (now University). Joe continued to excel in class and on the baseball and football teams. Before his sophomore year, however, Joe was drafted into the U.S. Army during World War II. He was honorably discharged in 1946 and returned to school. He graduated with a degree in education.

Although he was an outstanding pitcher and greatly desired to have a baseball career, the major leagues were closed to him. Instead, Joe Black became an effective pitcher for the Baltimore Elite Giants of the Negro Leagues for eight of his prime years. While Jackie Robinson broke the color barrier in 1947, it took years before black players were regularly accepted into the MLB.

In 1952, Joe Black was signed by the Brooklyn Dodgers, where he was Jackie Robinson's roommate. Joe experienced the same prejudice as Robinson and had to "turn the other cheek," as Robinson famously did. Despite the setbacks, he pitched well. The Dodger's manager, Charlie Dressen, said that Joe carried the team on his back to the pennant. Joe Black was named Rookie of the Year in the National League. And he was the first black pitcher to win a World Series game when the Dodgers defeated the mighty New York Yankees in the first game of the 1952 series.

When Joe retired from baseball in 1957, he turned down many lucrative corporate job offers to become a poorly paid teacher at my junior high school in our hometown. What Joe valued most was the respect of the students and faculty as a fine educator and the opportunity to be a positive influence in the school and the community.

That is when I had the good fortune to meet Mr. Black as his student, which started our lifelong relationship.

During these years and for the rest of his life, Joe Black was involved with the civil rights movement. He received the Martin Luther King Distinguished Service Award from Ms. Coretta Scott King in 1987. But despite his iconic status, Joe Black generously offered help and advice to me and other former students, as well as to many others. Dusty Baker, a highly respected Major League player and manager, said, "Joe always wanted to help and did not seek credit or accolades."

After seven meaningful and satisfying years of teaching, Joe Black accepted a job at Greyhound Corporation, in part so he could send his two children to college. Joe eventually worked his way up to vice president. After he retired, Joe continued to do a great deal of good work for others. His deeds are simply too numerous to record here.

When Joe Black passed away in 2002 at the age of seventy-eight, he was remembered with a celebration of his life at his church just down the street from what had been my father's automobile body shop. The old, spacious, and dignified Mount Olive Baptist Church was teeming with people. There were former teachers, sports figures, and countless community and church members in the audience.

Joe Black never name-dropped his friends. He would have protested the display in the corner of the stage. Set up were large stand-up photos of the man with Jackie Robinson, Roberto Clemente, Ken Griffey Jr., John H. Johnson, Greyhound CEO John W. Teets, Joe Garagiola, and his daughter and son, Martha Jo Black and Joseph "Chico" Black. Wonderful, loving speeches were given. Jerry Reinsdorf, the owner of the Chicago White Sox and the Chicago Bulls, delivered one tearful eulogy. I was honored to speak of Joe as a teacher and mentor. It was a fitting celebration of his meaningful life, a life suffused with civility.

Rule 60

BE NOT IMMODEST IN URGING YOUR FRIENDS

TO DISCOVER A SECRET.

A secret revealed is no longer a secret. Secrets revealed online can travel faster and further than ever before. But now as it was then, prying and urging others to pry into people's lives is thoughtless and uncivilized.

Rule 61

UTTER NOT BASE AND FRIVOLOUS THINGS

AMONGST GRAVE AND LEARN'D MEN, NOR VERY

DIFFICULT QUESTIONS OR SUBJECTS AMONG THE

IGNORANT, OR THINGS HARD TO BE BELIEVED.

STUFF NOT YOUR DISCOURSE WITH SENTENCES

AMONGST YOUR BETTERS NOR EQUALS.

Curb your tongue not only with the "grave and learn'd." As stated earlier, be certain to shield young and impressionable ears from bolts of profanity and thunderstorms of obscenity. The echo from a child's mouth is truly shocking.

Avoid pretense and do not speak above people's heads. Remain credible by not bringing up frivolous things. Plain speaking is still a virtue.

At the Hockey Game

One night our whole family was enjoying a live hockey game. We were part of a large, excited crowd that greeted the home team with roars of approval.

The game began with some brisk action. Not long into the first period, a loud voice from several rows behind yelled a stream of obscenities at our goalie. We all quieted down and listened in disbelief. The barrage of foul language continued.

A man one row behind us called out to the man who was uttering the profanities, "Hey, we didn't come to the game to listen to your foul mouth!" The man retorted, "I paid for a ticket just like everyone else. I can say whatever I want."

Though my wife was cringing, I stood up and turned around. "You are wrong," I said, pointing to the offender. "We are all here to enjoy the game, and we don't want to hear your filthy language—especially with our kids here."

The man glowered at me but his demeanor changed abruptly when virtually everyone in our section stood up, turned toward him, and voiced their agreement by yelling a hearty "shut up." It was a great feeling to have so many people have your back. Even in his drunken state, this man was intimidated into acting right for the rest of the game. He buttoned it up. And it was reassuring when event security came over.

When it is safe to do so, we must back each other up when it comes to violations of decent behavior. And we have an obligation to protect our children.

Rule 62

SPEAK NOT OF DOLEFUL THINGS IN A TIME

OF MIRTH OR AT THE TABLE; SPEAK NOT OF

MELANCHOLY THINGS AS DEATH AND WOUNDS,

AND IF OTHERS MENTION THEM, CHANGE IF

YOU CAN THE DISCOURSE. TELL NOT YOUR

DREAMS BUT TO YOUR INTIMATE FRIEND.

Even back then, no one liked a wet blanket. There is no substitute for good judgment in choosing the subject of a conversation. A splash of sadness and woe at a time of happiness can drown a happy crowd. Measure your words and tone before unleashing them. Note the emphasis in the rule on being upbeat at the table and redirecting those who insist on pulling a buoyant group down. This is when good-natured humor comes into play.

Rule 63

A MAN OUGHT NOT TO VALUE HIMSELF OF HIS

ACHIEVEMENTS OR RARE QUALITIES OF WIT,

MUCH LESS OF HIS RICHES, VIRTUE, OR KINDRED.

Modesty, one of the great virtues of the past, seems to have fallen out of favor. Wrap your good deeds and achievements in a cloak of understated cloth but persist in doing them. You need not be the "trumpet of your own virtues."

Value your attempts to be a good human being, raise your children to be civil, and make a clear distinction between riches of character and those of a baser, materialistic kind. "It is wrong to assume," John D. Rockefeller Sr. once said, "that men of immense wealth are always happy." Be pleased with the attributes and things you possess.

Letter to Martha Washington from Philadelphia on learning of his appointment as commander in chief of the American forces, June 18, 1775:

"SO FAR FROM SEEKING THIS APPOINTMENT I HAVE USED EVERY ENDEAVOR IN MY POWER TO AVOID IT, . . . ITS BEING A TRUST TOO GREAT FOR MY CAPACITY."

G Washington

Rule 64

BREAK NOT A JEST WHERE NONE TAKE

PLEASURE IN MIRTH; LAUGH NOT ALOUD NOR

AT ALL WITHOUT OCCASION; DERIDE NO MAN'S

MISFORTUNE THO' THERE SEEM TO BE SOME

CAUSE.

Do not laugh when another is suffering because of hard luck, even if it is self-induced. Timing is everything; don't joke when those around you are not in a jocular mood. Excessive and inappropriate laughter is unfeeling. The same goes when seeing people physically hurting themselves. Instead, see if they are okay and what help can be rendered.

Be especially careful when you joke over social media. Humor can easily be misinterpreted without the benefit of hearing a person's tone of voice and seeing that person's facial and body expressions. And gross and sick jokes, to cautiously use today's language, suck.

Rule 65

SPEAK NOT INJURIOUS WORDS, NEITHER IN JEST

NOR EARNEST; SCOFF AT NONE ALTHOUGH THEY

GIVE OCCASION.

We all know that words can hurt us. Do not hurl hateful verbal barbs at anyone, particularly children; they belie your maturity and confirm your incivility. Name-calling is to be avoided.

A joke at another's expense is a nasty deed, and on social media is especially cruel because of the potentially large number of people who may read it.

Restoring Self-Composure

Everyone had assembled for the house closing at the attorney's office. The buyers, the sellers, and the real estate agents were seated at the table with the settlement attorney who would conduct the transaction. The buyers and sellers in particular were understandably anxious.

In the middle of the proceedings, one of the sellers became agitated and, without saying why, rolled up a piece of paper and threw it in the direction of her agent. The room itself seemed in shock. The settlement attorney turned to the seller. Politely and in a soft voice, the attorney told the seller that, if there was an issue to discuss, they should talk openly about it in a civil and businesslike manner. Silence. The seller took in the tone and the words of the lawyer. After a long moment, the seller was able to calmly discuss the issue. The parties quickly resolved it and they were able to go on to complete the sale.

A quiet but responsive voice and a firm presence can bring responsible behavior back into a room.

Rule 66

BE NOT FORWARD [OBSTINATE] BUT FRIENDLY

AND COURTEOUS, THE FIRST TO SALUTE, HEAR,

AND ANSWER. BE NOT PENSIVE WHEN IT'S A

TIME TO CONVERSE.

Few of us are accused of being too friendly. Be friendly enough. The civil person puts others at ease by smiling, initiating friendly conversation, engaging people, and being responsive. And if you receive a text or e-mail with a request or a question, try to respond as soon as possible, even if it's to say you'll get back to the person as soon as you can at a later time.

It is generally nice to strike up a friendly conversation, but what of those awkward moments with a stranger on a plane, bus, train, park bench, or any public place? A greeting and a smile are always in order but start a conversation with a seatmate only if it seems welcome.

Rule 67

DETRACT NOT FROM OTHERS, NEITHER BE EXCESSIVE IN COMMANDING.

A civil person does not disparage, decry, or belittle but gives others their due and affords them their say. Respect your colleagues' styles and approaches as you would have them respect yours. Try to be an ensemble player on the stage of life. Avoid hogging the spotlight. Although it is easy to see yourself as the star of the show, remember that life is not a soliloquy. It is not all about "me."

Demanding Service

On what would ordinarily be a leisurely afternoon, I agreed to accompany my wife to the mall because the store we would be going to had extremely courteous and helpful employees.

The men's shoe department, which had a tremendous selection and knowledgeable salespeople, was having its semiannual sale. It was very busy and I was politely asked to take a seat until someone was free to help me.

My wife said she was going to the restroom. I looked around at the great variety of shoes as I waited my turn. Several salespeople were moving very quickly to customers with boxes of shoes stacked in their arms.

Suddenly, a man sitting in the row of chairs where we were all waiting raised his voice and yelled in the direction of a passing sales clerk, "I have been here for fifteen minutes and no one has waited on me yet!" The salesman stopped in his tracks and replied in a very polite tone, "We are trying, sir. I will be with you as soon as I possibly can." The complaining man then loudly responded, "I want service now!"

When the salesman came over to me at my turn, I offered to come back at another time. "No," he said. "I will take care of you now." I then threw caution to the wind, knowing a serious confrontation was unlikely to ensue in such an open, public place. I purposely raised my voice some and said something I knew the salesman could not say. "You have to deal with that complainer." I glanced in the direction of the loud, rude man.

Next, the man was towering over me. I stood up so that we were practically face to face. I was relieved to see that he was much shorter than me. There were several moments of silence. Looking him in the eye, I asked in a calm voice, "What are you going to do now?" He thought it over for a moment and then said, in a mild voice, "Nothing." He then returned to his seat and waited his turn.

Although the salesman could not challenge the impatient and demanding customer, I could at some risk. But I felt strongly that someone had to let the man know he had crossed the line of civility. My wife returned. Believe it or not, she liked the pair of shoes I had chosen.

Rule 68

GO NOT THITHER, WHERE YOU KNOW NOT WHETHER

YOU SHALL BE WELCOME. GIVE NOT ADVICE WITHOUT

BEING ASK'D AND, WHEN DESIRED, DO IT BRIEFLY.

It is not difficult to know when you are not welcome in a personal or social situation. Be sure your presence is desired before your foot crosses the threshold. Knowing if your advice is welcome is trickier. Like most of us, you believe your wise counsel should be sought.

Restrain from meddling, especially in family matters, unless your advice is solicited. If you are invited to do so, it is nice to lead with a gentle way of stating your opinion, like, "It seems to me that . . ." If you have no opinion, say so. If you want to stay out of the situation, say so.

Determining whether to offer your advice or opinion online is complex. Here's one ground rule: if you have not been given permission to follow a person but you can see that person's news feed, it is best to refrain from posting your opinion or advice on something that person has shared.

Rule 69

IF TWO CONTEND TOGETHER, TAKE NOT THE

PART OF EITHER UNCONSTRAINED AND BE NOT

OBSTINATE IN YOUR OWN OPINION. IN THINGS

INDIFFERENT BE OF THE MAJOR SIDE.

Perception varies with the view. Remember that another set of eyes has a different perspective. Your view is only one of many; a landscape seen through a telescope, kaleidoscope, or microscope assumes a unique aspect.

Honor a friend or anyone else by respecting that person's opinion, even if it differs from yours. If the issue is of little importance, let it go. Now really, how important is it to always be "right"?

Rule 70

REPREHEND NOT THE IMPERFECTIONS OF

OTHERS, FOR THAT BELONGS TO PARENTS,

MASTERS, AND SUPERIOURS.

Who are we to judge others? Empathize, don't criticize. As a
boss or coworker, as a friend, and as a parent, couch your censure
as well-intentioned, private, constructive criticism. You have
arrived as a truly civil person when you are no longer judgmental
of others.

Rule 71

GAZE NOT ON THE MARKS OR BLEMISHES OF

OTHERS AND ASK NOT HOW THEY CAME. WHAT

YOU MAY SPEAK IN SECRET TO YOUR FRIEND,

DELIVER NOT BEFORE OTHERS.

Control your curiosity and hold your tongue when it comes to the marks on other people's bodies. The same applies to people with physical disabilities. Do not avert your eyes, but do not stare. Both make a person self-conscious. Do not inquire. If you apply the golden rule, you will always be discreet with your comments.

Rule 72

SPEAK NOT IN AN UNKNOWN TONGUE IN
COMPANY BUT IN YOUR OWN LANGUAGE, AND
THAT AS THOSE OF QUALITY DO AND NOT AS
THE VULGAR. SUBLIME [LOFTY] MATTERS TREAT
SERIOUSLY.

It is rude to carry on a conversation in a language that is not
known to all present. This could also apply to inside jokes, which
are a language shared by friends. Try to refrain from them while
in wider company. And avoid jargon and abbreviations that others
may not be familiar with. Being left out is not a good feeling.

Rule 73

THINK BEFORE YOU SPEAK, PRONOUNCE NOT IMPERFECTLY NOR BRING OUT YOUR WORDS TOO HASTILY, BUT ORDERLY AND DISTINCTLY.

Sift your thoughts before serving them up; the dish will be far tastier to those who consume it. Measure your phrases carefully so they are clear in their meaning to those who receive them.

Thinking and listening before speaking applies to family, social, and business situations. You need not abandon spontaneity and sincerity. It takes only a moment to weigh the mode of the message as well as the message itself.

In other words, you should try to organize your thoughts before you open your mouth or share them on social media. Before you hit "Post" or "Send," read and reread what you have written. While spoken words may drift away, the digitally written word is forever.

Rule 74

WHEN ANOTHER SPEAKS, BE ATTENTIVE YOUR

SELF AND DISTURB NOT THE AUDIENCE. IF

ANY HESITATE IN HIS WORDS, HELP HIM NOT

NOR PROMPT HIM WITHOUT [BEING] DESIRED.

INTERRUPT HIM NOT, NOR ANSWER HIM TILL HIS

SPEECH BE ENDED.

"Listening 101" should be a required course at all stages of our education, beginning with preschool. As we would advance from one grade to the next, we would learn to be attentive, wait for the speaker to finish, and refrain from rudely interrupting the speaker for any reason.

Advanced students would be able to wait until a question is finished before beginning to answer it just in case the question did not end the way they thought it would. Some people gather their thoughts a bit more slowly than others. Consider that they may need a pause before making a response.

All good professional interviewers and members of the press hear people out and wait patiently for their turn to speak. In this way, they learn a great deal by listening carefully. "To listen well," former Chief Justice John Marshall said, "is as powerful a means of communication and influence as to talk well." Speaking of listening, it is significant and excellent that so many people are learning sign language in order to communicate with the hearing-impaired and that many speakers have a sign language person on the podium with them.

In the Courtroom

In the courtroom, Denise, a criminal defense attorney, was cross-examining the witness testifying against her client, the defendant, whom she believed had been falsely accused of robbery. The witness was confused about who might have committed the crime. Slowly she began to crumble under the questioning. Tears welled up in her eyes and streamed down her cheeks.

Denise was about to ask her another tough question. Instead, she paused, slowly approached the upset witness, and handed her several tissues.

We are all human beings. Even a lawyer during a critical moment in an important trial does not have to be unfeeling.

Rule 75

IN THE MIDST OF DISCOURSE ASK NOT OF

WHAT ONE TREATS, BUT IF YOU PERCEIVE ANY

TO STOP BECAUSE OF YOUR COMING YOU MAY

WELL ENTREAT HIM GENTLY TO PROCEED. IF A

PERSON OF QUALITY COMES IN WHILE YOU ARE

CONVERSING, IT IS HANDSOME TO REPEAT WHAT

WAS SAID BEFORE.

We've all experienced those mildly uncomfortable moments when someone joins a group immersed in conversation. That person should not expect a recap when coming into the middle of a discussion.

On the other hand, we all know what it feels like to want that recap. It is generous to extend this courtesy to someone who arrives later. The best solution may be to present a summary of what has transpired in the conversation so far.

Rule 76

WHILE YOU ARE TALKING, POINT NOT WITH YOUR

FINGER AT HIM OF WHOM YOU DISCOURSE, NOR

APPROACH TOO NEAR TO HIM WHOM YOU TALK,

ESPECIALLY TO HIS FACE.

"Get your finger out of my face!" As sad as it is to utter those words, imagine how rude the person is who provokes them. Physical proximity can be threatening and can produce a physical response. You should keep a proper distance when conversing with another.

Rule 77

TREAT WITH MEN AT FIT TIMES ABOUT BUSINESS,

AND WHISPER NOT IN THE COMPANY OF OTHERS.

Your business may be all-important to you and to some of those around you but know when and to whom it is of little interest. Be sure not to stir it into every conversation and situation. Do not assume your companion finds matters of commerce and industry suitable topics for the occasion or wants to soak up the finer details of your newest hobby.

The second part of the rule is plain and simple: whispering is an act of rudeness and an affront to those in your company. If you cannot speak the words to all present, stifle yourself.

Rule 78

MAKE NO COMPARISONS, AND IF ANY OF THE

COMPANY BE COMMENDED FOR ANY BRAVE

ACT OF VIRTUE, COMMEND NOT ANOTHER FOR

THE SAME.

Comparisons of people are usually a poor idea, save for in the world of professional sports. As difficult as it is, try to avoid comparing your children to one another or to other children. If it is done, it should not be in the presence of those children. Comparing peers' actions can be equally unwise. An exception would be if the comparison is undeniably harmless or in good humor.

As for the second part of the rule, an act of virtue or bravery should be singled out as special. Before you do so, make sure you have identified the right person.

Rule 79

BE NOT APT TO RELATE NEWS IF YOU KNOW

NOT THE TRUTH THEREOF. IN DISCOURSING OF

THINGS YOU HAVE HEARD, NAME NOT YOUR

AUTHOR. ALWAYS A SECRET DISCOVER NOT.

To reiterate: rumormongering, like gossiping, is a most uncivil enterprise. Talk is cheap because supply exceeds demand. Always verify a news story before commenting or sharing online. If it seems too outrageous or sensational to be true, that's probably because it isn't true. Avoid reading or watching only the news that reinforces your own worldview. False or exaggerated "news," like the seed of the nastiest weed, will take root and sprout. And it has an undeniable effect on our public discourse.

If you are privy to information of a sensitive nature, shield your source and be discreet in broadcasting it. Sound judgment in such matters is vital.

Your nose does not belong in another's tent. In other words, don't pry.

Rule 80

BE NOT TEDIOUS IN DISCOURSE OR IN READING

UNLESS YOU FIND THE COMPANY PLEASED

THEREWITH.

The long graduation speech usually bores us. Verbosity should be a misdemeanor. Discuss a matter crisply and exercise your sense of empathy to be sure you are not putting people to sleep.

Keep your electronic communication short and concise, especially at work. No one wants to find a novel in his or her inbox.

When Less Is More

Each year, a business professor I know announces to her class that a point that cannot be made in five minutes or less is not worth making. Her students often chuckle at the irony that a college professor, notorious lecturers that they are, makes this claim. Amazingly enough, she doggedly abides by this principle. She chooses her words sparingly. Believe it or not, she never does speak for more than five minutes on a particular topic.

This well-respected professor often challenges a student to lead the entire class on a particular topic, such as climate change, in a succinct way. In short, she teaches by setting the example.

Rule 81

BE NOT CURIOUS TO KNOW THE AFFAIRS OF

OTHERS, NEITHER APPROACH THOSE THAT

SPEAK IN PRIVATE.

Tending to your own life is a full-time job; sometimes it goes into overtime! How in the world do people find time to intrude on the lives of others? In our more civil world, there will be no room for nosy people or those who horn in on private conversations.

Rule 82

UNDERTAKE NOT WHAT YOU CANNOT PERFORM

BUT BE CAREFUL TO KEEP YOUR PROMISE.

Resist the urge to accept the pass when you know you cannot make it to the goal line. When we overcommit ourselves, we are likely to become anxious and fumble the ball. If you know you cannot score, say no. It is far better to refuse the handoff than to disappoint the team and lose the game. An exhausted player needs to sit out despite the urge to keep going.

A promise is to keep. Trust is based on performing on your promises. You should always be there when it counts. People rely on you, and you should be willing to make a personal sacrifice to meet your commitments.

When the peace treaty
with Great Britain was
finally signed, ending
the American Revolution,
George Washington was
fifty-one years old. Having
made the commitment to
command the troops, he'd
been in uniform more than
eight years. During that
entire period, he spent only
three days at his Mount
Vernon home. To keep a
promise, George Washington
believed in sacrifice. He lost
half his net worth during
the Revolutionary War.

Rule 83

WHEN YOU DELIVER A MATTER [MESSAGE], DO

IT WITHOUT PASSION AND WITH DISCRETION,

HOWEVER MEAN [LOW] THE PERSON YOU DO IT TO.

Be like the discreet mail and commercial carrier. Transfer the letter or package with a professional air. Say nothing, don't raise your eyebrows, and don't sneer.

Rule 84

WHEN YOUR SUPERIOURS TALK TO ANY BODY,

HEARKEN NOT, NEITHER SPEAK NOR LAUGH.

Eavesdropping—with intent or by accident—is a form of theft. Snoops and spies are not welcome in business, so don't attempt to listen to words not meant for you. Develop a mature professional attitude if you wish to get ahead.

Carefully choose whether to click "Reply" or "Reply All" to an e-mail when many people were included in the e-mail chain. Determine whether your reply is suitable for everyone included or just the original sender, then hit "Send."

Rule 85

IN THE COMPANY OF THOSE OF HIGHER QUALITY

THAN YOURSELF, SPEAK NOT TILL YOU ARE ASK'D

A QUESTION, THEN STAND UPRIGHT, PUT OFF

YOUR HAT, AND ANSWER IN FEW WORDS.

Times and manners change and so do we. Today we are all of the same quality and do not need to wait until spoken to. We need not be concerned about wearing a hat. We can afford the questioner the pleasure of a brief response.

Rule 86

IN DISPUTES, BE NOT SO DESIROUS TO

OVERCOME AS NOT TO GIVE LIBERTY TO EACH

ONE TO DELIVER HIS OPINION AND SUBMIT TO

THE JUDGMENT OF THE MAJOR PART, ESPECIALLY

IF THEY ARE JUDGES OF THE DISPUTE.

How tempting it is to raise our voices and overwhelm others in a dispute but consensus is still the best way to settle a controversy. There is nothing wrong with compromise.

Think of the early days of our republic and of the many signatures on the Declaration of Independence. Remember the Founding Fathers' emphasis on their collective intelligence. Follow their example of wisdom in gathering the facts, weighing the possibilities, and asking others for their opinions as you engage in the decision-making process. As we advance, we should also look back.

Now available are the tools of alternative dispute resolution, both arbitration and mediation. The use of these should be voluntary. They give us a more efficient and less confrontational way to resolve disputes.

When attempting to settle a dispute over an indirect medium, such as e-mail, make sure everyone has had a chance to respond before coming to a final conclusion. Consider setting a time limit for the response.

Rule 87

LET THY CARRIAGE [COMPORTMENT] BE

SUCH AS BECOMES A MAN: GRAVE, SETTLED,

AND ATTENTIVE TO THAT WHICH IS SPOKEN.

CONTRADICT NOT AT EVERY TURN WHAT

OTHERS SAY.

The word "carriage" comes from a bygone era and is archaic (as is the use of exclusively masculine references). A person's comportment or demeanor, however, does tell us much.

A serious, settled, and attentive person shows respect to those present, pays mind to what is being said, and does not arbitrarily contradict others. We would all do well to note our "carriage" now and then.

Rule 88

BE NOT TEDIOUS IN DISCOURSE, MAKE NOT

MANY DIGRESSIONS, NOR REPEAT OFTEN THE

SAME MANNER OF DISCOURSE.

Repeat after me: I will not repeat myself. I will not repeat myself. I will not . . .

You get the point: redundancy is an annoyance. And the tedious speaker runs the risk of losing the audience. "A bore," Henry Ford once said, "is a fellow who opens his mouth and puts his feats in it." So when you speak, stick to the point, pay attention to your vocabulary, and enthrall your listeners.

Rule 89

SPEAK NOT EVIL OF THE ABSENT, FOR IT IS

UNJUST.

Fairness is basic to our entire social system. Never speak ill of someone who is not present to mount a defense or to set the record straight. And remember: this rule applies to both analog and digital conversations; if you speak evil of someone over social media, it is there forever and can be inadvertently passed along to the subject. If ever there was a golden opportunity to exercise the golden rule, this is it.

From a letter to Joseph Reed, January 14, 1776:

"FOR AS I HAVE BUT ONE CAPITAL

OBJECT IN VIEW, I COULD WISH

TO MAKE MY CONDUCT COINCIDE

WITH THE WISHES OF MANKIND AS

FAR AS I CAN CONSISTENTLY."

G Washington

Rule 90

BEING SET AT MEAT, SCRATCH NOT, NEITHER

SPIT, COUGH, OR BLOW YOUR NOSE EXCEPT

[WHEN] THERE'S A NECESSITY FOR IT.

This one is child's play, or should be. Good table manners are always in order and should be second nature regardless of what is being served. When at the table, imagine a mirror before you and ask yourself if you would like to be the person sitting opposite. As in all matters of behavior, knowledge and execution are both important.

Rule 91

MAKE NO SHEW [SHOW] OF TAKING GREAT

DELIGHT IN YOUR VICTUALS. FEED NOT WITH

GREEDINESS. CUT YOUR BREAD WITH A KNIFE,

LEAN NOT ON THE TABLE, NEITHER FIND FAULT

WITH WHAT YOU EAT.

Relish your relish—but not to extremes. And don't gulp your meal in one . . . gulp. A piecemeal approach, such as cutting your food into small bits, can spread out the spread, and everyone can enjoy the time at the table. Chatting with your companions is a great way to slow yourself down.

Leaning is okay, though sitting up straight is probably more proper. But don't fret too much about the angle of your spine. Elbows should be off the table during the meal and not used to support you but it is not a sin to relax hands and arms on the table.

Be grateful for sustenance. Do not voice any complaints whatsoever.

Rule 92

TAKE NO SALT OR CUT BREAD WITH YOUR KNIFE

GREASY.

See how we have evolved! Still, today we must only remember not to double-dip our chips.

Rule 93

ENTERTAINING ANY ONE AT THE TABLE, IT

IS DECENT TO PRESENT HIM WITH MEAT.

UNDERTAKE NOT TO HELP OTHERS UNDESIRED

BY THE MASTER.

Vegetarian dinners are fine today. The point here is the importance of offering your guests the best you can afford. Do not serve your guests a meager meal. Be as generous as you are hospitable. The last comment in this rule refers to a less egalitarian time than today.

Rule 94

IF YOU SOAK BREAD IN THE SAUCE, LET IT BE NO

MORE THAN WHAT YOU PUT IN YOUR MOUTH AT

A TIME, AND BLOW NOT YOUR BROTH AT TABLE

BUT STAY TILL IT COOLS OF IT SELF.

Don't stuff, don't puff, and don't huff. Slurping should be reserved for the frozen confection or a hot bowl of soup. Of course, it is better to avoid slurping altogether if you can, but if you do it, apologize quietly. "Excuse me" should follow the involuntary acts of passing gas or burping as well.

Rule 95

PUT NOT YOUR MEAT TO YOUR MOUTH WITH

YOUR KNIFE IN YOUR HAND; NEITHER SPIT

FORTH THE STONES OF ANY FRUIT PIE UPON A

DISH NOR CAST ANYTHING UNDER THE TABLE.

Cut with your knife, but eat with your fork. A fork and spoon are the preferred utensils for delivering food to the mouth.

Spitting is still frowned upon and is totally unforgivable at the table. Pits can be removed from the mouth with a napkin. At a picnic, spitting while eating watermelon is okay, as long as you aim far away from your companions.

How many of us have secretly given food to the dog under the table? It's best to avoid tossing scraps under the table—even if you know a furry companion is ready to clean up after you.

Rule 96

IT'S UNBECOMING TO STOOP MUCH TO ONE'S
MEAT. KEEP YOUR FINGERS CLEAN AND, WHEN
FOUL, WIPE THEM ON A CORNER OF YOUR TABLE
NAPKIN.

It is okay to bend over slightly when eating your food but it's best
not to give the impression of loading gravel into a dump truck.
Although the days of finger bowls are past, the need for clean
fingers at the table is not. Use your napkin, not the tablecloth or
your clothes. And always, always wash your hands before serving
or eating food.

Rule 97

PUT NOT ANOTHER BITE INTO YOUR MOUTH TILL

THE FORMER BE SWALLOWED. LET NOT YOUR

MORSELS BE TOO BIG FOR THE JOWLS.

Don't wolf down your food. Your stomach will more easily digest the food that you have chewed. Even a mighty hungry eater should spare dining companions the view of an unsightly stuffed mouth. A glutton is never welcome as a tablemate or guest.

Rule 98

DRINK NOT NOR TALK WITH YOUR MOUTH FULL,

NEITHER GAZE ABOUT YOU WHILE YOU ARE

DRINKING.

At the very least, consider the possibility of choking while trying to talk as you eat and drink. This rule, which has been with us for at least 250 years, protects us against more than the charge of poor manners. Your companions may not be skilled in the Heimlich maneuver or CPR. You may look around as you drink unless your aim is affected, causing a slip between the cup and your lip.

Rule 99

DRINK NOT TOO LEISURELY NOR YET TOO HASTILY. BEFORE AND AFTER DRINKING, WIPE YOUR LIPS. BREATHE NOT THEN OR EVER WITH TOO GREAT NOISE, FOR IT IS UNCIVIL.

Drink it up or drink it down, but time it right. As stated earlier, do not slurp. Be cautious if only to save on laundry bills. As you imbibe your beverage, breathe softly and quietly. Loud breathing is like loud talking. And there is never a good reason for it except while doing yoga, meditating, or catching your breath. Bear in mind, however, that an emergency medical situation often starts with loud, unexplained breathing.

Rule 100

CLEANSE NOT YOUR TEETH WITH THE TABLE

CLOTH, NAPKIN, FORK, OR KNIFE, BUT IF OTHERS

DO IT, LET IT BE DONE WITH A PICK TOOTH.

Toothpicks may have been the tool of choice back then but today using one to clean your teeth in public is considered a bit crude (and it's bad for your gums and teeth). Wait until you're in private and whip out your favorite dental floss, or wait until you get home. All dentists say to floss only those teeth you want to keep. This good habit will cut down on nasty dental visits and it's been strongly linked to your overall health. Thank goodness wooden teeth are a thing of the distant past.

Rule 101

RINSE NOT YOUR MOUTH IN THE PRESENCE OF

OTHERS.

Some acts should only be done in private.

Rule 102

IT IS OUT OF USE TO CALL UPON THE COMPANY

OFTEN TO EAT. NOR NEED YOU DRINK TO

OTHERS EVERY TIME YOU DRINK.

Breaking bread has long forged the bonds of friendship—but it isn't necessary to eat and drink every time you get together with friends or family. But do offer.

Rule 103

IN THE COMPANY OF YOUR BETTERS, BE NOT

LONGER IN EATING THAN THEY ARE. LAY NOT

YOUR ARM BUT ONLY YOUR HAND UPON THE

TABLE.

It's nice to keep pace with your dining companions. Again, there is no such thing as "betters." And to reiterate: keep those elbows off the table during the meal but it is really not a big deal to rest your hands or arms. Maybe the chair has arms for yours.

Rule 104

IT BELONGS TO THE CHIEFEST IN THE COMPANY

TO UNFOLD HIS NAPKIN AND FALL TO MEAT

FIRST. BUT HE OUGHT THEN TO BEGIN IN TIME

AND TO DISPATCH WITH DEXTERITY, THAT THE

SLOWEST MAY HAVE TIME ALLOWED HIM.

As tempting the smells and as hungry the stomach, the mannered guest awaits the host to begin the meal. The host, in turn, should not try the patience of the guests. If the host says to go ahead, it really is okay to begin. If the food is hot or warm and the host cannot immediately sit down at the table, the host should insist that everyone start. Remember the napkin goes on the lap first, and "host" is a gender-neutral term.

Waiting in Line

Jill was inching up in a long line at the fast-food restaurant. Suddenly, a new order taker stepped up to a new cash register, caught her eye, and said, "Ma'am, I'll take your order over here." Although it would have been easy to step to the front of a new line after being invited to do so, she replied, "The gentleman in front of me hasn't been helped yet either." With a grateful smile, the man in front of Jill shifted the small child he was holding in his arms, said thank you to her, and moved to the front of the new line.

Rule 105

BE NOT ANGRY AT THE TABLE, WHATEVER

HAPPENS, AND IF YOU HAVE REASON TO BE SO,

SHEW [SHOW] IT NOT BUT PUT ON A CHEERFUL

COUNTENANCE, ESPECIALLY IF THERE BE

STRANGERS. FOR GOOD HUMOUR MAKES ONE

DISH OF MEAT A FEAST.

A scowl is an inappropriate facial expression at the table. "Anger is never without reason," Benjamin Franklin said, "but seldom with a good one." Put on a pleasant face and muster up high spirits. Humor is the key. A happy band of diners enhances every meal. And, of course, it does not have to be meat.

Rule 106

SET NOT YOURSELF AT THE UPPER SIDE OF

THE TABLE, BUT IF IT BE YOUR DUE OR THAT

THE MASTER OF THE HOUSE WILL HAVE IT SO.

CONTEND NOT, LEST YOU SHOULD TROUBLE THE

COMPANY.

A place for everything and everyone: the well-mannered guest does not sit in the host's seat unless asked to do so. Sit where directed by the host or anywhere if the host says so.

Rule 107

IF OTHERS TALK AT TABLE, BE ATTENTIVE, BUT

TALK NOT WITH MEAT IN YOUR MOUTH.

Talking with your mouth full was a serious transgression, especially in the 1700s. Like rule 98, this rule applies to all food and focuses on a most distasteful practice.

As previously noted, aside from the risk of choking, it is just plain gross to talk with a stuffed mouth. And no one can understand what you are saying. Concentrate on the conversation rather than solely on the food in your mouth.

Rule 108

WHEN YOU SPEAK OF GOD OR HIS ATTRIBUTES,

LET IT BE SERIOUSLY AND WITH REVERENCE.

HONOUR AND OBEY YOUR NATURAL PARENTS,

ALTHOUGH THEY BE POOR.

Respect religion if you are a believer, and recognize that it has often provided for decency, civility, and good character. An individual can, of course, be civilized without being religious. The same goes for being spiritual without being religious. It should be noted that the teachings of many religions have inspired many to engage in charitable endeavors and service to others.

Honoring and obeying your parents and grandparents, whether biological or not, is the rule if they love and respect you and take good care of you. It may be difficult when you have differences of opinion with them but those differences should not be the source of dishonorable treatment.

Some children are inclined to snarl and snap at their parents most disrespectfully for a period of years (hint: preteens and teenagers), but most come through those difficult times to finally appreciate the guidance, support, and love their parents gave them and continue to give. The same goes for grandparents. This appreciation often happens when the children become parents and it should be gratefully communicated.

Rule 109

LET YOUR RECREATIONS BE MANFUL, NOT SINFUL.

If only every human could live by this rule . . .

Rule 110

LABOUR TO KEEP ALIVE IN YOUR BREAST THAT

LITTLE SPARK OF CELESTIAL FIRE CALLED

CONSCIENCE.

The final rule points us in the direction of the source of all rules, our conscience. It is aptly referred to in the rule as the spark that must be kept alive. If your fire is extinguished, your compass is gone and you will lose your way on the trail of life.

Learn to know and appreciate the difference between right and wrong. Then do the right thing no matter how large or small. "To see what is right and not to do it," the ancient philosopher Confucius said, "is want of courage."

Do the right thing no matter the circumstances. The contemporary American historian and professor, Jon Meacham, astutely stated this: "The war between . . . what's right and what's convenient, between the larger good and personal interest, is the contest that unfolds in the soul of every American." Do it even if it is unpopular. Do not bow to peer pressure. Be willing to sacrifice to do the right thing.

Many acts of conscience are concerned with large and important matters of a serious nature. But many more are the tiny opportunities that life presents to us each day. Big or small, dramatic or ordinary, we must keep our spark of conscience alive and put others before ourselves.

At the Gym

Even the most casual and simple act of civility can enhance your life and the lives of others. A woman who was working out at the gym asked the desk attendant for aspirin. She had a bad headache. He said they had just run out.

A man within earshot offered to go out to his car to get some. The woman told him there was no need. Despite her protests about the wintry weather, this gentleman jogged out to his car in his shorts and T-shirt, drenched in sweat and right in the middle of his workout. He quickly returned with a small bottle of pills. The grateful woman thanked him.

The man thought nothing of it. He was simply doing the right thing.

TEN OTHER CIVIL THINGS YOU CAN DO

Treating others with a high degree of civility goes hand in hand with your own positive feelings toward life. These ten suggestions, which supplement Washington's rules, may help bring you a greater sense of being plugged into life.

1 THINK OF YOURSELF AS A HUMAN BEING FIRST. Many people identify themselves in terms of their jobs: dentist, lawyer, carpenter, auto mechanic, teacher, computer analyst, homemaker, and so on. Try thinking of yourself first as a person who just happens to work in a certain area. If you view yourself in this way, you are likely to develop a stronger sense of empathy with other people. Remember the thread of common humanity that runs through all of us and the capacity we have to find it in each other. We are all in this life together.

2 BE TOLERANT OF OTHER PEOPLE. At the very foundation of a civil society is tolerance. Being tolerant sounds easy, but it takes effort. Prejudice is the child of ignorance. It is an unfavorable opinion or feeling formed beforehand without knowledge, thought, or reason. Shake off old prejudices. Work on your ability to allow for differences in the way other people perceive the world, speak, and act. Welcome and applaud diversity. It adds value to our lives. It contributes to the well-being of our country. This is how we broaden our horizons. Abraham Lincoln once said, "I don't like that man. I must get to know him better."

3 ATTEND FAMILY GATHERINGS. Your family is a constant in your life that provides lifelong identity and a sense of self and security. When you stay in touch with your family, you maintain bonds with people who stabilize your life. You have history. The close family engenders love.

4 STAY ABREAST OF THE NEWS. Keep in touch with events and politics in your neighborhood, your region, your state, your country, and the world. A sense of community is one of the building blocks of a civil world. Read newspapers, follow the news online, turn on radio and television news with differing points of view and, importantly, neutral stations like public broadcasting. Attend meetings, conferences, and political debates to keep informed. It is difficult to be aware of all that is happening, but it is important. And it is the duty and privilege of everyone to vote.

5 JOIN A CIVIC ORGANIZATION. To connect to those in your immediate community, lend your efforts to a civic organization. You will join people who are involved in furthering the common good through charitable undertakings. Participants in civic organizations and the growing number of civility groups, clubs, and associations get acquainted under the best of circumstances: a joint effort to improve the lives of others and the goodness of your community and, thus, the nation.

6 TAKE UP GARDENING. It's America's number one hobby for a reason. Being in touch with nature is satisfying. As you dig and till the soil and encourage plants to produce nature's bounty, you feel in harmony with the earth. You appreciate the change of seasons and the weather—the rain, snow, and sun—and the interdependence of all living things. It is another way to increase sensitivity to all who inhabit this good earth.

7 PARTICIPATE IN A TEAM SPORT. Choose a sport and a level of play that suits you. In addition to developing a sense of camaraderie with your team members, you will make enduring friendships that go beyond game time. A team that imparts good values, a spirit of trying your best, good sportsmanship, and healthy exercise can give you a wonderful outlook on life and a real sense of belonging.

8 DANCE. Every type of dance can give you an enhanced feeling of life. You connect with others when you move in rhythm to music. Dancing with a single partner or joining a group in a line or circle dance gives you a unique feeling of being alive. If you don't know how, you can learn. Listening to music is a great activity to share with others. Playing an instrument in a band or orchestra gives collective pleasure. Music is a language of its own that has universal appeal. It is also a great escape.

9 VOLUNTEER. By giving time, effort, or possessions— including donations—to help others, we help ourselves. Recognize the ways in which you can contribute to the lives of other human beings. Be involved in a homeless shelter, food bank, school, camp for the underprivileged, or other charitable activity. Support the important work of the worthwhile non-profits. You will find their actions are meaningful and satisfying. Consider joining or volunteering for organizations whose sole purpose is to help people or animals.

10 PROTECT THE ENVIRONMENT. As you work to improve the environment, you bring yourself closer to the human community. An appreciation of life should include respect for the earth. Join in conservation efforts and recycling endeavors. Be environmentally aware as you live your life. We are the custodians of the planet, not just for ourselves but also for future generations. Our stewardship must be relentless and enduring.

A LAST WORD

Civility starts with you. As you work toward practices of greater empathy, courtesy, and consideration, see how your life improves. Watch the effects expand and touch the lives of others. If enough of us engage in civil practices and encourage them in others, the pendulum will swing in that direction.

This book is intentionally apolitical because civility is a universal concept. Anyone has the potential to be an angel or a brute, regardless of party. But all should take heed, including poll-watching politicians. They will realize that they must be civil in order to be elected.

Just as a stone thrown into a pool of still water creates ripples in ever-spreading, concentric circles, so does the practice of civility affect society. But like those watery ripples, the effect dies down unless the effort continues. We would all like to live in a more civil world. We must act to make that world a reality.

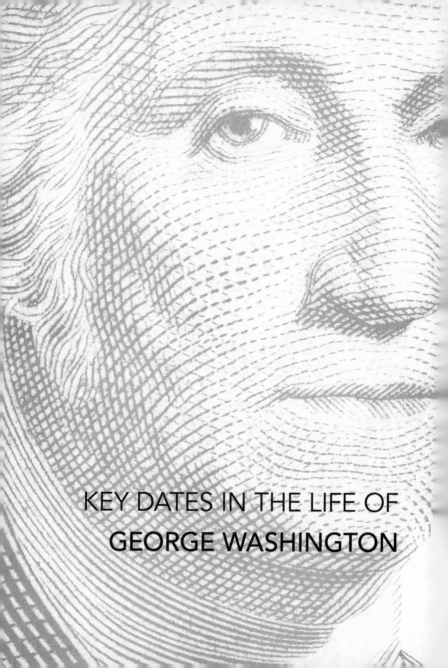

KEY DATES IN THE LIFE OF
GEORGE WASHINGTON

- **1732** Washington is born on February 22 in Westmoreland County, Virginia.

- **1743** His father Augustine, whom he reveres, dies.

- **1746** At age fourteen, Washington writes down 110 rules under the title *Rules of Civility and Decent Behaviour in Company and Conversation*.

- **1749** Washington is appointed surveyor for Culpeper County, Virginia, and goes on his first survey expedition.

- **1753** Robert Dinwiddie, acting governor of Virginia, sends him to the Ohio Valley to warn the French that they are encroaching on British territory, an admonition they ignore.

- **1754** Promoted to lieutenant colonel, Washington is dispatched to a fort where Pittsburgh now stands to help guard it against the French, who defeat him at Great Meadows, Pennsylvania.

- **1755** After resigning his commission and returning to farming in 1754, Washington is chosen to join the staff of British general Edward Braddock during the French and Indian War. During the Battle of Monongahela, he fights bravely but unsuccessfully against the French, Abenaki, Lenape, and Shawnee.

- **1755** Returning unhurt to his Mount Vernon home, Washington is shortly made commander in chief of the Virginia militia by the governor.

- **1758** Leading a successful campaign against the French as they retreat, Washington then retires from the military.

- **1759** Washington marries Martha Dandridge Custis, a young widow, manages their properties, and serves in the Virginia legislature, the House of Burgesses.

- **1761** Washington inherits Mount Vernon.

- **1774** Washington is a delegate to the First Continental Congress in Philadelphia.

- **1775** Sent as a delegate to the Second Continental Congress, Washington is unanimously elected commander in chief of the American forces.

- **1783** After leading his troops successfully in the Revolutionary War, he retires again to Mount Vernon.

- **1787** Washington emerges from retirement to attend and preside over the federal convention, at which thirty-nine delegates from twelve states sign the Constitution.

- **1789** Washington is unanimously chosen as the first president of the United States. He runs without party affiliation (none existed yet).

- **1793** Despite having drafted his resignation, Washington reluctantly agrees to run for reelection, in part to bridge deepening political divides. He wins unopposed. While many demand his coronation, he instead gives power back to the people, creating the first peaceful transition of power in our democracy.

- **1796** He publishes *George Washington's Farewell Address.*

- **1797** After refusing to serve as president again, he returns to Mount Vernon.

- **1799** Two months before his sixty-eighth birthday, on December 14th, George Washington dies at Mount Vernon. His final words are, "'Tis well."

ACKNOWLEDGMENTS

F ew books result from the efforts of one person. This one is no exception. I owe thanks to many, beginning with my wife, who is my model of civility. Adrianne is always other-directed and empathetic, selfless and kind, tactful and caring. Her kind parents, Walter and Betty Heafitz, were truly civil people and wonderful in-laws. Adrianne's parents and my parents, Nathan and Florence, reinforced my belief that civil behavior begins at home.

My sister Karen and my brother-in-law, Norman Leopold, must be counted among the very civil. The same goes for my sister-in-law, Debbi, and brother-in-law, Harvey Heafitz. I am grateful to our sons, Ethan and Elliott, and their wives, Natalie and Brooke, for their support. Natalie's mother, Judy Royal, also deserves recognition for her help. Brooke's mother and father, Kelly and Peter O'Hanley, made major contributions to this book and have a high civility quotient. Alix Brown has been very supportive.

I would like to further acknowledge Gail Wingate and Alison Heafitz for their substantial contributions to this project.

Both Gail and Alison took time from their busy lives to educate me as to appropriate conduct and the dangers involved in the use of social media. And the resourcefulness of cousin Jon Heafitz has been of enormous help. Heather Wurzer has also proved herself indispensable, generously offering her considerable skills and winning attitude. Mike and Penne Baer have given me valuable technical support. Other contributors include Dave and Carol Romer, Heidi and Carl Wurzer, Raymond Castillino, Curt Combar, Mary Beam, Char Lyon, Jennifer Clary, Jeanette O'Malley, and Angela Delaplaine.

I am pleased that the team at Andrews McMeel Publishing saw fit to publish this book—both the original edition, *By George! Mr. Washington's Guide to Civility Today*, and the version you hold in your hands now, which substantially updates, revises, and builds on the book I wrote nineteen years ago. Very importantly, I would like to acknowledge with great thanks Patty Rice, executive editor at Andrews McMeel. She has always been enthusiastically supportive, and we share the belief that we must improve the level of civility in our country. She welcomed this book with open arms, for which I am very grateful.

Great thanks must go to Kevin Kotur, my talented editor on this revised edition. He calls himself a "word nerd," but he is much more than that. Kevin's advice was invaluable throughout this process, offering excellent improvements to my manuscript. His good nature, patience, and sense of humor are much appreciated. Kevin is a civil person who shares my view that the pendulum can swing back to greater civility.

I am also excited to work with Susannah Greenberg, a truly gifted, civil, and successful book publicist. To have an impact, a book must be promoted in many ways; Susannah's professionalism, enthusiasm, and wide-ranging skills are a blessing.

It has been my good fortune to learn many lessons in civility from a diverse range of people. The least I can do to repay them is to recognize them here, in these extended—but nevertheless appropriate—acknowledgments. I am still learning and trying not to stray from their examples.

Walter Mills is one such example. His civility encompasses his constant desire to help people. Every time I sit in his barber's chair, I get an education. Walter's good deeds are innumerable. He expects nothing in return, not even a thank you. Walter finds his acts of kindness and consideration to be satisfying in and of themselves.

There are many other people I would like to thank for demonstrating civility in action. They are Cliff and Eda Viner, Noah and Michelle Leopold, Susan Meisler, Marianne and David Halpin, Jim and Amy Morris, Todd and Elycia Morris, David Mandelbaum, David Wingate, Rachel and Dave King, Michael Heafitz, Bob and Michelle Byrd, Carolyn and Pete Leyon, Tom Lynch and Carlys Kline, Joe and Nancy Stanfield, Larry and Kathy Walker, Phil and Jan Swinson, Joe and Jeannie Popovich, Richard and Jakie Lewis, Steve and Kathy Janowitz, Albert and Esther Perry, Teresa Schrift, Brian Murray, Jerri Shafran, Dick Bernstein, Sharon Mulholland, Kraike Williams, Simor Moskowitz, and Kelly Magruder. Like many of us, I have learned a great deal from our sweet dog, Chloe. I am trying to be as patient as she is.

Other people who have taught me about acting civilly are Joan and Jack Canterbury, Mary McGuigan, the late Ralph, Jim, and Bill Miller, the late Harvey Steinberg, Robert and Marcia Rosenberg, Bob and Nancy Leins, Regina Tenali, Hedy and Amir Farazad, Mark and Beth Egber, Jean Marie Apa, Dr. Harshit Agarwar, Dr. Anna Sidor, Jessica Biggs, Samantha Koontz, Kristen Palm, Elizabeth Wilson, Connie Wantling, Mike Corrigan, Ed Jewell, and Kathy Osborn.

Among role models, I should also mention Bob Royal, Paul and Natalie Royal, Craig and Leigh Royal, Dora Vega, Dr. Rebecca Herman-Smith, Dr. Mary James, Dr. David Yu, Dr. Everett Hart, Dr. David Kossoff, Dr. Elizabeth Guardiani, Dr. Stephen Reich, Dr. Sandeep Bagla, Dr. Eddie Phisuthikul, Lorrie Lynch, Dr. Conrad Bakker, Dr. Thu Pham, Dr. David Levine, Dr. Wayne Xue, Dr. Morse Davis, Dr. Muneeb Malik, Dr. Kevin Hackett, Dr. Grant Louie, Dr. Paul DeMarco, Dr. Emma DiLorio, Dr. Nathan Deckard, Eddie Goldstein, Bobby and Susie Barth, Eddie and Lane Nemeth, Alan Feinberg, Steve Gladchuck, Matt Rosenheim, Ian Harding, Dr. Gloria Eng, and Ellen DeGeneres, for her constant reminder: "Be kind to one another."

Other fine people whose civility has influenced me are Geoffrey and Andi Zola, Robin and Danny Morris, Paul Morris, Margaret Klaff and her late husband, Sonny, Esther Ain and her late husband, Michael, Steve and Harriet Shapiro, Julian and Diane Spirer, David and Sharon Spiegel, the late Cal and Bobbie Chizever, my neighbors Alaina and Greg Dale, Allan and Gayle

Carlson, Cary Hobson and Cindy Mann, Mark and Connie Nagy, Al Cameron, Maryland State Trooper David Ryan, Lisa Berriola and David Viertels, Mary and Ed Giblin, Linda Ramos, Kumi and Jerome Maultsby, Dr. Michael Davis and his wife, Carly, Poppy and Christopher Archer, and Jane Ryan.

Additionally, these other practitioners of civility have had an effect on me. They are Barb Strauss, Jane Silberberg, Jason Ditto, Sarah Powers, John Morris, Sally and Betsy Heafitz (maiden names), Gilbert and Naomi Bass, Mort Heafitz, Louis and Ina Heafitz, David and Kayo Heafitz, Lewis and Susan Steinberg, Wayne and Carol Leadbetter, Annie Cummins and Lou DiPasquale, Jeff and Judy Bouie, Gail and Jim Colen, Bob and Kathy Pellicot, Theresa Bradbury, Lisa Stuart, Karen and Tom Lewis, Joe Nussbaum, Janie Culos, Gary Llum, Dr. Brent Berger, and postal carrier Brian Sullivan.

There are still others who deserve recognition for acting with teachable civility. They are Marlene England, Brittany Grimm, Diane Branson, Spencer Cummings, Bob Michael, George Shadoan, Frank Coviello, Joe D'Erasmo, Mike and Betsy Bell, George Cholakis, Bob Meier, Michael and Renee Sussman, Ron and Jennie Olson, Joe Anselmo, John and Randy Severt, Judge John McAuliffe, the late Judge Jim McAuliffe, Chief Judge Robert Bell, Tom and Linda Harmon, Allison and Josh Siegel, Jason Weber, Randy King, the late Dr. P. M. Forni, and Danny Wegman.

Other people who show the way are Courtney Austin, C.J. and Erin Soschin, Jay and Jesse Gerard and Donelle, Joy Ceesay and her husband Kebba, Cheryl and Todd Pearce, Maria and Brian Kramer, Irene LeClair, Judy Neches, Hunter and Mary Payne, Pat Payne, the late Herb Payne, Debra Powell, Wes and Katherine Powell, Emily Parkhurst, Dave Pasti, Al Frederick, the late J. D. Grewell, Scotty Scafidi, Dr. Emily Rogell, Stanton and Dotty Samenow, Yeshvant and Jean Talati, Atul Thakkar and his wife, Riva Zohar, Ven Richardson, Pam Zusi, and Barbara and Alan Pickholtz.

Additionally, there are Judge Marybeth McCormick, Judge Ann Harrington, Judge Ann Albright, Judge Steven Johnson and his wife, Pat, Judge Charles Day, Judge Peter Messitte, Judge Irma Raker, Judge Robert Greenberg, Judge Dennis McCurdy, Judge Larry Beard, Michael Banks, Judge Eric Johnson, Doug Fauth, Pete Reckendorf, Linda Cohen, Billy Hardy, Saadia and Tehsin Ghaffar, Randy Greenberg, Ann and Michael Cohen, Robin and David Grover, Karl and Pat Johnson, and Steve Gittelson.

Lastly, the following people have also set an example worth adopting: Steve and Beth Santa Maria, Jerry Reinsdorf, Sandy Koufax, Martha Black, Chico Black, Bridgette Greer, Mitch Albom, Jon Meacham, Doris Kearns Goodwin, Jon Bramnick and his wife, Patricia, Brian and Pam Canham, Paul and Rosemary Lamond, Judy Madden, Heather Gifford, Samantha Czibur, Suzanne Iacovelli, Tamya Pauley, Dez Johnson, Noah Daly, Rory Chalcraft, Jhulan Bowie, Michelle Forbes, Jennie Jamison, Mark Knott, Jen Felice, Angela Vasquez, Asyah West, the late Nikki Phelps, Larrissa Hudson, Morgan Davis, Valerie Bodnar,

Renee Mann, Colin Gilsdorf, Kelly Jones, Crystal Grimsley, Bob Englert, Mal Snyder, Kathy Grad, Elizabeth Chung, Judge W. Milner Roberts, Judge Theresa Adams, Judge John Cejka, Judge Janice Rodnick Ambrose, Judge Julie Stephenson, Joe Krebs, Barbara Harrison, and the late Jim Vance.

I am grateful to all of those people whose names I have included in these acknowledgments. For any people I have inadvertently omitted, please accept my apologies.